Nowcasting The Business Cycle

A Practical Guide For Spotting Business Cycle Peaks Ahead of the Crowd

James Picerno

Beta Publishing

Published by Beta Publishing, LLC
www.CapitalSpectator.com
caps@CapitalSpectator.com
+1.732.710.4750

Nowcasting The Business Cycle:
A Practical Guide For Spotting Business Cycle Peaks Ahead of the Crowd

ISBN-13: 978-1492923855
ISBN-10: 1492923850

To Liz and the girls, my guiding lights

Since all models are wrong the scientist cannot obtain a "correct" one by excessive elaboration. On the contrary following William of Occam he should seek an economical description of natural phenomena. Just as the ability to devise simple but evocative models is the signature of the great scientist so overelaboration and overparameterization is often the mark of mediocrity.

Since all models are wrong the scientist must be alert to what is importantly wrong. It is inappropriate to be concerned about mice when there are tigers abroad.

— George E. P. Box
"Science and Statistics," *Journal of the American Statistical Association*,
December 1976

Contents

Acknowledgements

This book is yet another attempt to stand on the shoulders of giants and summarize and interpret some of the research and empirical facts in the vast realm of business cycle analysis. Accordingly, I owe a major debt of gratitude to all the economists and analysts (some of whom are listed in the bibliography) who've made contributions over the decades in trying to unravel the great mystery that's commonly known as boom and bust.

I'm also grateful for many discussions with Robert Dieli, an economist at NoSpinForecast.com who has shared his deep knowledge of economics with me in recent years. In addition, the editors in my various journalism projects with macro and markets have earned my enduring respect and gratitude in allowing me to publish variations on this book's main theme. Thank you Evan Simonoff at *Financial Advisor*, Wendi Webb at HorsesMouth.com, and the editorial staff at Saxo Bank's TradingFloor.com. Thanks also to Tim Argenziano and Dan Strachman, two invaluable resources (and great friends).

Finally, my family has been an inestimable source of energy, support and encouragement in the many hours I've spent writing, researching and editing. Thank you Elizabeth, Pamela, and Alison. And for my mom, Eva, my first teacher and my enduring inspiration.

Preface

There are many victories worthy of celebration in the field of macroeconomics. Banishing the business cycle to the dustbin of history isn't one of them.

Periods of economic contraction are inevitable, or as close to inevitable as anything in the world of macro can be. Enlightened policy by central banks and governments may be able to minimize the damage by restricting recessions to brief, relatively mild episodes. But the wisdom of anticipating even a limited degree of triumph in the war against the business cycle is debatable—again—after the Great Recession of 2007-2009 reordered expectations by reminding the world that old hazards die hard.

Some say that this is simply the nature of capitalism: boom and bust are as endemic to free-market economies as snow is to winter. Yet many economists insist that recessions can be engineered away, or at least strangled down to a manageable, low-level hazard—if only policymakers would make informed decisions. Maybe, but history isn't kind to this brand of optimism, at least not so far. Governments have tried any number of techniques over the decades to test theories in the real world. So far the results are, well—let's be generous and describe this history as mixed. The future may be different, but the case for thinking so still relies on wishful thinking rather than hard evidence.

Recessions, for reasons that aren't fully understood, persist... despite the best-laid plans of economists and policymakers. That leaves two critical and forever-topical questions: When will the next slump strike, and how bad will it get? This book is concerned only with the first question. That's more than enough to keep us busy. Searching for answers, or at least robust estimates of the potential for trouble, is among the more practical of pursuits in the sphere of economic analysis. If we can improve our appraisal of the fluctuating odds of recession risk, even slightly, we'll be in a stronger position to prepare for the next storm and keep the fallout to a minimum.

Yes, there are already countless books on dissecting the economy, including a small library of titles that promise to unlock the secrets of predicting the twists and turns in the business cycle. Do we really need another one? Yes, for several reasons. First, the pages ahead concentrate exclusively on estimating recession risk in something approximating real time—soon after a contraction has started, which is to say before the downturn has inflicted the heaviest damage on your investments, your business, your career. Note the term "soon after." We'd all like to know when a recession is coming before it's arrived. Alas, that's not possible (despite what you may have heard) and so we must settle for the next-best strategy.

In other words, don't confuse the analytics on the pages ahead with forecasting so much as interpreting the economic numbers as currently published. The book in front of you is dedicated to developing and exploring a simple but effective method of assessing the economy's vulnerability to contraction. Fortunately, we have a rich database to study and a long line of research to guide us.

Doesn't a "simple" model doom us to failure? Not necessarily. "Just as the ability to devise simple but evocative models is the signature of the great scientist so overelaboration and overparameterization is often the mark of mediocrity," the statistician George E. P. Box wrote.[1]

The world is awash in sophisticated analytics that win awards, impress economists, and dazzle the intellect. But complexity and reliability aren't always natural companions in the dark art of dissecting the business cycle, which has deceived more "experts" than any other phenomenon in the dismal science. But our quest isn't hopeless, at least not entirely. For all the mistakes and misguided analyses, economists have still made progress in recent decades in probing the broad swings in the economy and so we'll not be shy in embracing the available research when it helps us see the big-picture trend in clearer terms.

In any case, the stakes are certainly high. The business cycle is the main risk factor that drives success and failure in quite a lot of what unfolds in the modern world of business, finance and our personal lives as it relates to money and wealth. It's not the only hazard, of course, but it's an important one and sometimes it's the dominant one, for good or ill. The old saying on Wall Street that genius is a bull market is an exaggeration, but there's quite a bit of truth there. And the lesson applies well beyond money management. Whether you're an individual investor watching over your retirement nest egg; the owner of a small business on Main Street; a manager running a billion-dollar pension fund; or a CEO in charge of a global corporation, we're all in the same boat: a large portion of triumph and defeat is closely bound up with the broad swings in the economy.

It's fair to say that the next recession may be the single-biggest complication for your career, your investments, your net worth, and so much more. Recognizing this truism means that we all need to spend more time thinking about and preparing for the dark side of economic destiny. The business cycle is the mother of all known (and recurring) risk factors. It's essential that we focus on developing a process for assessing the likelihood of the threat. We need a reliable, timely warning system that's relatively uncomplicated and transparent.

The business cycle looms large for everyone, individually and collectively, and it's a positive influence... most of the time. The economy, after all, is usually growing. But sometimes it's shrinking. We ignore the cycle's capacity to reverse course every so often at considerable peril.

Some critics protest that trying to analyze the business cycle on any level is always condemned to failure. It certainly can be—if you're trying to achieve the impossible. Efforts at forecasting the state of the economy for, say, six months or a year down the line are subject to a black hole of unknowns. No wonder that the track record generally for predicting economic activity is so poor. That's hardly a shock. No one can see the future, and so it's inevitable that even the smartest economists are regularly surprised.

A slightly more prudent (or less dangerous) approach is the focus of this book, and it can be summed up as follows: routinely read the economy's signals (based on the latest numbers) and determine, as early as possible, when there's a high probability that the economy has already slipped over the edge, or is in imminent danger of doing so. That may sound like a trivial advantage, but most people—

---

[1] Box (1976), p. 792.

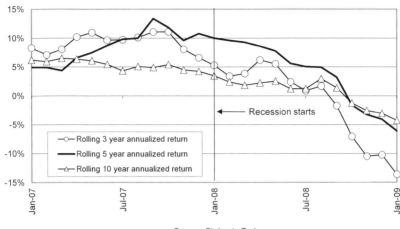

Figure A.1
S&P 500 Rolling Price Returns, monthly, based on month-end data

Source: St. Louis Fed

including many economists—don't fully recognize when a recession has started until the deterioration is obvious. By that point, the prime window of opportunity has probably closed for taking defensive measures in your personal accounts, your business, your portfolio, your career. But if we can learn the techniques for recognizing a cyclical downturn's presence relatively early—soon after it's begun, or just as it's starting—we'll have an advantage that tends to elude most folks.

The good news is that there are effective methods for assessing the current state of the business cycle—methods that provide timely warnings of when the economy has started rolling over to the dark side. This isn't forecasting; instead, it's recognizing when a majority of critical indicators have turned the corner overall. I call this nowcasting, or predicting the present, you might say. Or maybe we should call it backcasting, a reference to developing a sober view of what's just happened.

Why do so many analysts miss these turning points until well after the storm has started raging? There are many reasons, although one is the tendency to forget that recessions creep up on us, like the proverbial thief in the night. If you're not looking closely for the telltale signs of this party crasher, and doing so in a systematic, intelligent manner that's grounded in empirical research, you'll likely miss the warning signs of the early stages of economic decline. This point is often lost in the din of debate about the economic numbers du jour and fuzzy memories about what happened the last time the economy tanked.

Even if you're looking closely, it's essential to focus on a carefully selected and representative sample of data. No less critical is analyzing the numbers across time horizons that are long enough to minimize the short-term statistical and seasonal noise.

Quite a lot of people are under the impression that by the time a recession hits, it's too late for defensive action. That may be true in some cases, but it's far from a universal rule that applies to all economic slumps. Looking for a recession to declare itself, in convincing quantitative terms via published reports, quite often presents a chance to prepare for the worst that's yet to come.

Consider the Great Recession. According to the official estimates from the National Bureau of Economic Research, January 2008 was the first full month of economic decline. By the spring of that year, the numbers were clearly showing that the economy was in trouble and that a new recession was already in progress. But hadn't the window of opportunity already closed at that point for taking defensive action? Not necessarily.

As one test, let's compare how the stock market's trailing returns played out during the 12 months before and after the Great Recession began (Figure A.1). The ample gains that prevailed before the economy stumbled didn't suddenly evaporate in the early months of 2008. As a result, recognizing early on—even as late as May or June—that a recession had started still left investors with a brief period to preserve a fair amount of any gains earned in the previous years.

Looking at a variety of economic indicators also reminds us that the Great Recession's pain didn't arrive as an across-the-board bolt out of the blue in January of that fateful year. For instance, retail sales and new orders for durable goods held up surprisingly well during the first half of 2008 (Figure A.2). Although both series weakened as the year progressed, the recession's initial bite was relatively mild compared with the carnage that followed.

The window of opportunity for defensive action, once a recession begins, can and does vary considerably. But it's hardly the case that all of the damage is invariably front-loaded. That may be true for some financial indicators or certain sectors of the economy in some recessions, but it's far from an iron rule. In other words, developing a relatively reliable methodology for recognizing when a contraction has recently infected the broad economy in conspicuous terms represents a powerful piece of strategic information. But there's a catch: You have to be looking, and the search requires an analytical lens that's different from the usual tools that are deployed for *predicting* recessions. Yes, life would be much easier (and more profitable) if we anticipated recessions. But since no one can reliably muster such powers of prophecy, nowcasting is the only dependable game in town.

∞

The forces that unleash recessions typically arrive quietly, building slowly, and spreading across various corners of the economy until the descent becomes broadly detrimental and patently obvious. As I discuss in the following chapters, cyclical tumbles are usually the byproduct of deterioration that's built up in multiple parts of the economy—a decay that progressively deepens and expands, gradually reaching a tipping point of terminal decline. The problem is that during the initial period of decay it's easy to be deluded into thinking that all's well if you're unsure of what to look for, or if you're not looking at a broad set of key indicators through an appropriate statistical lens. But beware: there's a huge amount of economic data to digest and most of it's irrelevant, if not misleading, in the search for early, reliable signs of recession risk.

Looking to the usual suspects for guidance isn't much help. For example, newspaper reports and the standard economic analytics aren't usually productive

Figure A.2
Retail Sales and New Orders For Durable Goods (in millions $)

Source: St. Louis Fed

resources for making strategic decisions about the risk of a new downturn. In fact, if you listen to commentary from the wider world, you're sure to be whipsawed with conflicting interpretations on every new data point. Quite a lot of what you'll read or hear is short-sighted, mistaken, and downright wrong. Historical perspective is essential for evaluating the business cycle, but you'll have to dig deep to cut through the noise.

The news media, of course, is focused on headlines, drama, and how the number du jour relates to last month or the previous quarter. It's also obvious that the analysts making the boldest claims tend to receive the most attention. News without proper context, however, tends to be deceptive at major turning points for the economy. It may be entertaining, but it's not terribly helpful.

As for professional economists, a fair amount of the analytical efforts in the field are focused on projecting next month's (or the next quarter's) industrial production, unemployment, and so on. But quite a lot of this research is of limited value, if any, for estimating recession risk. Dismal scientists too often miss the forest for the trees. Keep in mind, too, that some economists may have a political axe to grind, particularly when a new election is approaching and it's in their candidate's interest to promote (or attack) the macro trend of the moment.

Objectively analyzing recession risk, in sum, is a highly specialized discipline. But because recessions are relatively rare, there's minimal demand for this line of intelligence... most of the time. The few analysts who've mastered this specialty are in short supply, especially when their services are needed most: at the tail end of a long period of economic growth.

The task ahead, then, is working harder to identify those points when the cyclical clues are truly flashing red—and, no less important, figuring out when they're not. The solution, in principle, is straightforward. Identify a range of the most productive cyclical signals, study the historical track records, and use the relevant studies in the research literature as a guide for developing a simple but effective process for analyzing incoming data in real time.

Doesn't the economic profession already do this? Some analysts rise to this standard. But there's still plenty of room for improvement, for reasons that will become obvious over the course of this book.

Remember, too, that even flawed methodologies are going to be right some of the time. But a system that suffers a high degree of false readings is hardly salvaged because it was right the last time.

The main goal is developing a model for generating high-confidence recession-risk signals. That's a high standard. But compared with a lot of what's already out there, it's possible to move closer to this ideal, if only on the margins, in part because the competition on this front is generally unsatisfying.

Fortunately, some of the solutions for developing robust signals are uncomplicated, such as focusing on year-over-year trends to avoid the seasonal complications that can bedevil monthly reviews. Annual changes also help manage revision risk to a degree. Most economic reports are revised and so the initial estimates may be erroneous. Accordingly, it's necessary to look at a range of key indicators to minimize the possibility that we're being misled by the first cut of numbers. Another essential task is de-emphasizing forecasting per se; instead, concentrate on judging recession risk based on the data in hand—nowcasting. We can also look for corroboration with our conclusions from several of the published benchmarks that track broad economic activity.

How do we know where to begin and where to look? Researchers have supplied us with a broad guidelines through the decades. Even so, it's easy to get sidetracked. With so much data available in the 21st century, and so many studies and analysts forecasting this or that, the risk of losing perspective is considerable in the miasma of information. The solution is to focus, focus, focus on the specific challenge of estimating recession risk.

Some aspects of this challenge can't be resolved. We still can't see around economic corners, no matter how hard we try or how much data we crunch. It's an obvious point, but it still trips up analysts on a regular basis. The aim on the pages that follow is developing a high degree of assurance for recognizing when a new recession has started. That still requires a few assumptions about the immediate future. But the risk of error is considerably lower compared with the standard techniques if we're looking for dependable signals about what's recently changed. That's a big difference compared with predicting what may (or may not) happen in the months ahead.

The primary source for thinking that we can do better is that researchers have continued to peel away the haze for recognizing when a new plunge has started. We may be long past the point of new discoveries that radically alter our ability to analyze recession risk. But the accumulated wisdom in macro analysis has inched onward, albeit in fits and starts.

Ultimately, we must focus on what's essential, and ignore everything else. Most of us simply want to know when the odds of a new recession are relatively high. If there's a hurricane coming, a bit of an advance warning that the storm is heading our way can be enormously helpful. But we must always be sensitive to the possibility of mistaking what appears to be a genuine threat when in fact it's only noise or a temporary soft patch. Indeed, a system for predicting recessions that's deeply flawed and prone to false alarms is worse than no system at all.

Finally, some readers may wonder why I don't also analyze the techniques that are the counterpart to assessing recession risk, namely: looking for signs of a new expansion after an economic contraction has run its course. The short answer: anticipating a fresh bout of growth is considerably easier than searching for new slumps. The main clue for the next expansionary phase is the existence of a recession already in progress. When the economy's shrinking, that's been a reliable—virtually infallible—sign that a new upturn is approaching. True, there's quite a bit of mystery about when, exactly, a recession will end and a subsequent rebound will start. In any case, that's a subject for another book and, to be fair, it's a less-problematic issue than looking for recessions. It's the short-term interruptions in the expansionary trend that create so much trouble, in part because they come as a surprise for so many people. The good news is that we can do better with minimizing the surprise factor.

Growth, meanwhile, prevails in the long run and so our task is somewhat easier for anticipating the sunny side of the cycle. History is tenacious in reminding us that there's probably a revival in the offing whenever the economy is suffering. I don't want to diminish the real-time challenge of deciding when a new recovery is near. That's still a tough act to pull off when a recession has us by the throat. On the other hand, there's only so much one can fit into a single volume.

In any case, analyzing recessions is enough of a challenge on its own. Growth, by comparison, can (and usually does) take care of itself.

Introduction

In February 2004, a rising star at the Federal Reserve delivered heartwarming news at the winter meeting of the Eastern Economic Association. The business cycle had been tamed, the speaker advised. "One of the most striking features of the economic landscape over the past twenty years or so has been a substantial decline in macroeconomic volatility," Ben Bernanke explained. The implication: recessions had become a diminishing threat to the body economic. Downturns arrived less frequently and when they did bite the pain was modest compared with their predecessors. The trend wasn't limited to the United States, the future chairman of the Federal Reserve said. The Great Moderation, as he called it, was smoothing the rough edges of economies the world over.[1]

Prevailing conditions at the time supported Bernanke's analysis. In fact, many analysts concluded that a new era of economic tranquility had dawned. But as the world was reminded during the Great Recession of 2008-2009, which started just four years after Bernanke's speech, the received wisdom in macroeconomics has been known to suffer a limited shelf life as a practical guide for thinking about the future.

The dark side of the business cycle slips into hibernation most of the time, perhaps due to enlightened policy—or luck? Yet the Bernanke in 2004 wasn't shy about giving the Federal Reserve a healthy dose of credit for the apparent change for the better in the macro climate. "My view is that improvements in monetary policy, though certainly not the only factor, have probably been an important source of the Great Moderation," he said.[2]

History, however, suggests that economic slumps (like rats and cockroaches) are virtually immune to clever extermination plans. That doesn't deter macroeconomists, who endeavor to figure out why economies stumble and how future downturns can be restrained if not avoided altogether. The source of the economy's to and fro through the decades has been attributed to everything from sunspots to blunders by central bankers. The Marxist interpretation simply warns that capitalism is inherently unstable and so a steady run of turmoil is fate. No matter your view on Karl and his political legacy, his defeatist view isn't too far from the truth, or so the historical record seems to indicate.

Such narratives are only the beginning, of course. You could spend the better part of a lifetime cataloguing the spectrum of theories that claim to uncover the reasons for the business cycle's persistence. But don't confuse an abundance of explanations with enlightenment. Despite countless studies intent on finding the truth, it's still debatable if anyone truly understands the big picture. Perhaps that's why recessions are a recurring menace.

In any case, the slumps keep coming, as they have for more than two centuries, and there's no reason for thinking that the future will be any different. "I devoutly hope our next downturn won't come for quite some time, but it surely will come

---

[1] "Remarks by Governor Ben S. Bernanke. At the meetings of the Eastern Economic Association, Washington, DC, February 20, 2004. 'The Great Moderation'": www.federalreserve.gov/BOARDDOCS/SPEECHES/2004/20040220/default.htm
[2] Ibid.

eventually," noted Richard Fisher, president of the Federal Reserve Bank of Dallas, in 2011.[3] As macroeconomic prophecies go, that's a keeper.

Recessions are no closer to extinction in the 21st century than they were in 1950—or 1850. Some say it's simply the essence of capitalism, or human nature's influence over matters economic. It's been the same whether it's an economy linked to a gold standard or fiat monetary systems; with or without a central bank running the show. The use of heavy regulation vs. something closer to a free-market ideal doesn't matter much either in terms of affecting the durability of broad economic fluctuations.

Macroeconomic theory may not have a satisfying answer for why these events roll on, but the profession isn't a total bust. Dismal scientists have learned a thing or two about economic volatility over the years. The future's still uncertain and always will be. It's safe to say that there's never a shortage of analysts who are caught napping at the start of a new downturn. Yet it's shortsighted to ignore the advances in recession analytics because some economists didn't recognize the warning signs the last time around.

Attitude Adjustment

Imagining a world that delivers steady progress toward kinder, gentler economic cycles seemed as plausible in 2004 as it is absurd today. Yet the Great Moderation was no illusion. Bernanke and the legions of economists who agreed with him weren't delusional in that halcyon period, before the worst recession in 80 years struck in early 2008. Ahead of that fateful slump, economic volatility *did* moderate and recessions *did* retreat in frequency and magnitude. The mistake was thinking that the trend heralded an era of permanently diminished macroeconomic risk.

It's hardly the first time that economic volatility was underestimated by the experts (nor is it likely to be the last). In 1960, the economist Arthur Burns, one of the 20th century's early pioneers of macroeconomic analysis, declared that "the business cycle is unlikely to be as disturbing or troublesome to our children as it was to us or our fathers."[4] In the following decade, Burns would eat those words. Appointed chairman of the Federal Reserve in 1970, he led the central bank through the turmoil of the 1973-1974 recession, the deepest up to that point since the Great Depression of the 1930s.

Perhaps it's human nature to think optimistically, a habit that eventually colors expectations for even the most objective of dismal scientists. Nonetheless, the business cycle endures. As of 2014, there have been 33 recessions since 1857, according to the National Bureau of Economic Research, the official score keeper of turning points in the U.S. economy. No one can afford to assume that this ignominious tally won't continue to climb in the years ahead, yet hope springs eternal.

Before the Great Recession, macroeconomists were congratulating themselves on the long stretch of shallow and infrequent recessions. And for a time, it looked

---

[3] "Speech by Richard W. Fisher. Washington, D.C., March 7, 2011. 'Churchill, Baruch, Lindsay Lohan, Congress and the Fed.' Remarks at the Institute of International Bankers Annual Washington Conference":
dallasfed.org/news/speeches/fisher/2011/fs110307.cfm#n1
[4] Burns (1960), p. 17.

like the business cycle had been conquered. But it all came crashing down in 2008. The arrival of the deepest recession in nearly a century has challenged the notion that economic risk can be engineered down to a manageable level through enlightened policy. Everything works in macroeconomics until it doesn't. Topics long considered settled terrain have recently been revived for a new generation of debate and research. Students of economic history will find parallels in contemporary discussions with the dialogues of the 1930s that included such luminaries as John Maynard Keynes, Friedrich von Hayek, and Irving Fisher. What's old is new in macro.

But let's keep our criticism in perspective. There's precious little opportunity for experimental research in macroeconomics. Testing the validity of one theory vs. another in a controlled setting is impossible. There are no laboratories to run trials and sort out the results. There's only one historical sample to dissect and it's burdened by a limited data set, questionable rules for interpretation, and an excess of mitigating circumstances. Even when new and presumably improved economic policies are implemented, it's never entirely clear if there's a direct connection between the adjustment and the economic outcome. There are too many moving parts in a modern economy to isolate specifics in the search of cause and effect to speak authoritatively.

That leaves economists to argue over the ideas that appear credible. But debates about theory aren't easily resolved, if at all, by studying history. The business cycle unfolds slowly and there's always doubt if the historical period in question is an exception to the rule, or even representative of how the system works generally. Indeed, this is a profession that still fiercely debates the catalysts of the Great Depression—more than eight decades and countless studies after the fact.

It's fair to say that consensus isn't about to break out in macroeconomics anytime soon. Perhaps the closest thing to harmony is the acceptance that economic output rises and falls through time. If we're inclined to emphasize what's conspicuous and beyond debate, we can agree that the cycle has the capacity to be something other than gentle at times. The inherently dynamic nature of capitalism endures, as Schumpeter warned, delivering a "perennial gale of creative destruction" through the course of history.[5]

If we must plead some level of ignorance for explaining why there's a cycle, much less curing it, we should still respect and study it, if only for self-defense. We can start with an easily confirmed fact, albeit one that's too often ignored: fluctuations in the broad economy persist. That's clear when looking backward. The problem, of course, is gazing ahead.

Inference & Error

Consistently predicting the timing of recessions with pinpoint accuracy is impossible, but that doesn't mean there's no hope for recognizing when the odds of a new downturn are elevated. Much of what's been uncovered in the art/science of anticipating and recognizing recessions falls into the empirical corner of economics. History suggests that under condition x, there's a higher likelihood of y. Economic theory helps us understand why there's a relationship—or, why we should be

---

[5] Schumpeter ([1942] 1950), p. 84.

skeptical of a relationship that appears to be relevant. Meanwhile, econometrics provides the tools for crunching the numbers and estimating the dynamic aspect of risk. If you need definitive answers and precise timetables, you're out of luck. But if we relax our expectations a bit, there's room for optimism about what can be achieved.

History isn't a consistently reliable guide for what happens next, of course. No amount of statistical analysis can wipe away the perennial mystery about tomorrow. But quantitatively based risk estimation can help recognize the hazards that look particularly threatening at a given point in time. Recessions rarely if ever strike without some type of warning. History doesn't repeat, but it's been known to rhyme.

Even the Great Recession wasn't all that unusual, aside from the depth of the downturn. The main set of factors that led to previous recessions conspired to bring us the 2008-2009 slump, according to professors James Stock of Harvard and Mark Watson of Princeton—two veterans of deciphering macro fluctuations. They found that "the same six factors which explained previous postwar recessions also explain the [start of the Great Recession]...." In particular, oil, monetary policy, productivity, uncertainty, liquidity/financial risk, and fiscal policy were the key elements:

> Within the context of our model, the recession was associated with exceptionally large movements in these "old" factors, to which the economy responded predictably given historical experience. While there were new events and exceptional policy responses in the 2007 Q4 recession, the net effect of these new events and responses was not qualitatively different than past disturbances—just larger. We interpret these results as pointing towards a confluence of large shocks that have been seen before, not towards new shocks that produced unprecedented macroeconomic dynamics.[6]

In other words, we've seen this movie... several times. You can never really prove anything in economics, but it's hard not to notice the recurring features that accompany boom and bust across the broad sweep of history—stylized facts, as they're called. "We have been here before," a pair of economists wrote in an expansive review of financial crises through the centuries. "No matter how different the latest financial frenzy or crisis always appears, there are usually remarkable similarities with past experience from other countries and from history," advised professors Carmen Reinhart and Kenneth Rogoff in their empirical masterwork *This Time is Different: Eight Centuries of Financial Folly*.[7]

The naïve assumption is that recessions are random events that arrive with no warning—economic acts of God. If true, attempts at recognizing the conditions that lead to these events are doomed to failure. But as research by Stock and Watson, Reinhart and Rogoff, and many other economists suggest, the prospects are in fact encouraging for evaluating recession risk as it rises and falls. Why? Because there's a recurring aspect to the economic conditions associated with slumps. The historical record clearly shows that economies don't suddenly, inexplicably shift from growth to contraction overnight. Recessions typically take time to fester, and the festering is almost always visible... if you're looking at the relevant indicators through a

---

[6] Stock and Watson (2012), p. 2.
[7] Reinhart and Rogoff (2009b), p. xxv.

practically designed analytical prism. It's not a perfect, symmetrical rise and fall; in some cases the deterioration arrives faster or slower compared with previous events. But the cyclical aspect of the process is noticeable if we monitor multiple indicators and aggregate the changes through time.

Good thing, too, since ignoring the business cycle is a luxury that few of us can afford. Recession risk drives many if not most of the hazards that bedevil individuals, businesses, governments and society in general. We can't neutralize this risk, but we can at least prepare for it when the storm clouds look particularly menacing. The only thing worse than a recession is a recession that arrives as a complete surprise. Fortunately, we can reduce the chances of finding ourselves in a state of ignorance by reading the cycle's tea leaves.

Whether we'll take advantage of what's been uncovered on this front is another matter. Consider the signals from the Treasury market's yield curve. It's usually a sign of trouble in those rare instances when interest rates on short-maturity securities rise above long rates—an inverted yield curve, as it's called. Inverted curves have dispatched early and generally accurate warnings about recession risk since the 1960s. No one should assume that this signal alone will tell us all that we need to know going forward. The yield curve may fail us the next time. The same can be said of any one indicator, no matter how impressive its track record. A responsible review of recession risk demands a broad review of indicators.

Still, when a predictor with an encouraging history flashes red, it deserves respect. "For over two decades, researchers have provided evidence that the yield curve, specifically the spread between long- and short-term interest rates, contains useful information for signaling future recessions," a 2009 study noted. A useful sign, but "despite these findings forecasters appear to have generally placed too little weight on the yield spread when projecting declines in the aggregate economy. Indeed, we show that professional forecasters are worse at predicting recessions a few quarters ahead than a simple real-time forecasting model that is based on the yield spread."[8]

Perhaps the inclination to question the timeliness of even the strongest warnings of macro trouble is part of the human condition of embracing optimism, which is especially tempting when recession risk is generally higher, i.e., after a long period of growth. It seems that living through the good times can cloud our capacity for critical analysis. It's now understood that our brains are susceptible to exaggerating recent experiences when anticipating the future. Cognitive biases bedevil us, according to the pioneering research from psychologists Daniel Kahneman and Amos Tversky. Their analyses show that it's psychologically difficult to accept the idea that the recent past may be a poor guide to the near term.[9]

We all want to believe that the good times will roll on. That's understandable, but it's a habit that's sure to become dangerous every so often. Growth dominates in the long haul and so expecting more of the same fares pretty well as a general outlook. But that expectation is destined to be wrong at some point. Overlooking our tendency to downplay future turning points leaves us vulnerable to large negative

---

[8] Rudebusch and Williams (2009), p. 492.
[9] See, for example, Kahneman and Tversky (1973), Tversky and Kahneman (1974), and Kahneman (1999).

surprises. That's no trivial issue when you consider that recessions usually start during the best of economic times.

There are plenty of other factors bedeviling the search for reliable clues about the business cycle's current state. Institutional biases, for instance, can skew the best guesses of professionals. Jeffrey Frankel at Harvard's Kennedy School of Government demonstrated that official government forecasts in 33 countries showed a tendency for overstating the case for economic growth.[10] Politics may play a role, too. At least two studies found that the International Monetary Fund's forecasts of growth were higher than the levels implied with basic economic evaluations.[11] Maybe that's not entirely surprising in the wake of reports that revealed that accuracy alone isn't always the sole or even primary motivation behind some macroeconomic predictions.[12]

Nowcasting Recession Risk

Even if we avoid the obvious pitfalls, it's easy to see the situation as bleak. History, after all, is littered with failure when it comes to business cycle analysis. But let's not sink into defeatism. In contrast with Dante's reaction when he approached the gates of hell, we needn't abandon all hope. In fact, we start with a considerable advantage in knowing that there's probably another recession out there somewhere. The real challenge isn't predicting when it will arrive so much as developing solid intuition for recognizing when the threat is exceptionally high. Progress on the latter will provide insight into the former. The work begins by focusing on the tools and techniques that will tell us when a downturn has recently started. Forecasting may be a fool's errand in economics, but looking for early indications that the cycle has entered the danger zone is something else entirely.

The distinction between predicting and nowcasting drives the logic of this book. That is, evaluating recession risk based on the latest economic indicators as opposed to predicting how the numbers will stack up down the road, which invariably runs up against a familiar obstacle: uncertainty. That doesn't mean we should always and forever refrain from forecasting. A disciplined, well-designed methodology of estimating what looks likely in the near-term future can be productive. But the world is awash in such efforts, and the results overall aren't terribly encouraging, which is why we need an alternative to the standard approach.

There are two basic ways to wrestle with recession risk. One is to forecast it; the other is to develop a high-confidence assessment of whether it's currently squeezing the economy. The world is teeming with guesses about the future, and they come with all the usual caveats. It doesn't help that some fatally flawed systems are occasionally accurate. Even if you're skilled at figuring out who's truly talented on this front—no mean feat—the uncertainty problem remains sizable. By contrast, identifying the start of major downturns in the economy in real time, using what we know today instead of what we think will happen tomorrow, is far less precarious (if the process is intelligently designed).

Eventually, all becomes clear... if you wait long enough. The gold standard on this front is the National Bureau of Economic Research's official announcements on

---

[10] Frankel (2011), which includes a bibliography of related studies.
[11] Aldenhoff (2007) and Dreher, et al. (2007).
[12] See Lamont (2002) and Laster, et al. (1999), for instance.

the dating of recessions. Because NBER is striving for a high level of accuracy that will stand the test of time, these announcements arrive well after the fact. The cyclical peak of December 2007, for instance, was identified 12 months after the recession started.[13]

The advantage of the slow-moving NBER methodology is that you don't have to worry about revisions. When the group says the cycle peaked, it's virtually certain that they're right and that everyone will agree with the conclusion today, tomorrow, and in the years ahead. But must we wait so long for clarity? The tradeoff in the pursuit of more timely signals is that earlier calls on cyclical peaks may suffer with accuracy. The earlier you declare a peak, the higher the possibility that you could be wrong.

The challenge is figuring out how to keep a lid on error while making relatively high-confidence assessments—as early as possible. It wouldn't hurt if the process that brings us closer to this optimal sweet spot is transparent, intuitive, and draws on free, publicly available data. Highly parameterized models with lots of moving parts, by contrast, may impress folks in academia. But the record on complex systems isn't terribly encouraging in business cycle analysis.

All of which inspires searching for a reasonable compromise that concentrates on timely judgments of the key economic variables. That's an inherently subjective task, but it's essential for interpreting the business cycle's patterns. The true business cycle, after all, is unobservable—it's a concept, an idea, rather than one number or a single index. We can see the outcome of what we call the business cycle through the synchronized movements of various economic metrics—employment, industrial production, consumer spending, etc. The true underlying source (or sources) that drive the synchronization, however, is a debatable topic at best. The most we can hope for is calculating a reasonable proxy that captures the economy's broad fluctuations. Decades of research offer a guideline, but there's no substitute for getting our hands dirty with the numbers. The economic gods have left mere mortals with the unpleasant work of conducting trial-and-error tests to figure out what is, or isn't, relevant.

Our handicap is sizable but it's not overwhelming, as we'll discover in the chapters ahead. There are no short cuts that will transform us into oracles, but standing on the shoulders of giants in the field of economic research can lead us to a useful group of indicators that dispatch relatively reliable warnings of when the economy is susceptible to a new round of contraction—particularly when we look at these indicators in a holistic manner, as opposed to the natural tendency to focus on a handful of numbers one at a time.

Overall, there's reason to think that 1) we can identify broad deterioration that's already in progress in the economic cycle; and 2) do so earlier relative to when the crowd recognizes that another downturn has become destiny. We can start by adjusting expectations based on key lessons uncovered by economic researchers and focusing on what's probable—as opposed to reaching for the stars by fooling ourselves that we can know what will unfold in the future.

---

[13] NBER issued a press release on Dec. 1, 2008 that stated: "The committee determined that a peak in economic activity occurred in the U.S. economy in December 2007": www.nber.org/cycles/dec2008.html

We also have an edge that wasn't available to previous generations: access to the numbers. It's no small advantage that economic data is now plentiful and quite a lot of it is published on the Internet. What's more, you can often find what you're looking for at no charge. In addition, economists have made substantial progress in mapping the connections between the various indicators and so there's greater opportunity for interpreting the data and using it wisely.

Keep in mind too that anticipating the risk of a general economic contraction is a somewhat easier task compared with the professional economist's burden, which is often one of routinely predicting everything from the future path of industrial production to the economy's quarterly gross domestic product. The goal on the following pages, however, is considerably less ambitious but far more practical: identifying those times when the odds appear elevated that a new recession has started.

"Most recessions remain undetected until they are well underway," noted a 2009 International Monetary Fund study that reviewed forecasters' track records.[14] Another review of predictions from private and government forecasters for the 20 years through 2006 concluded that "if past performance is a reasonable guide to the accuracy of future forecasts, considerable uncertainty surrounds all macroeconomic projections...."[15]

Surely we can do no worse than the average forecaster, although with a bit of effort it's possible and perhaps even likely that we can do slightly better. By focusing on the relevant data and using economic research to develop a simple but intuitive model to assess recession risk, we have a good chance of modestly enhancing our strategic intelligence. Given what's at stake, even a small degree of improvement will bring substantial advantages.

A degree in medicine isn't required for making informed decisions on health matters and you don't need years of training in meteorology to recognize when there's a storm coming. Similarly, intelligent evaluation of recession risk isn't solely dependent on holding a Ph.D. in macroeconomics. That's no slur against dismal scientists—some of my best friends are formally trained economists. But let's face it—monitoring the mother of all risk factors is too important to be left to "the professionals."

That's an invitation for us to take some responsibility for thinking clearly about recession risk. The motivation requires no explanation. As the American engineer C. F. Kettering reportedly said, "My interest is in the future because I am going to spend the rest of my life there."

Chapter Outlines

The rest of the book is a journey—a journey of exploring how we can develop a deeper understanding of the business cycle in order to identify, as early and confidently as possible, those times when a recession is upon us. The model isn't particularly complicated—feel free to skip ahead to the final chapter for a summary

---

[14] Loungani and Tamirisa (2009), p. 3.
[15] Reifschneider and Tulip (2007).

on how to assess recession risk—but it is practical and, so far, has proven to be quite valuable in quantifying the big-picture trend.

To understand what's behind it all, you'll want to review the chapters that precede the strategic finale. Chapter 1 offers a short review of the evolution of business cycle analysis. Although economic research that's been published in recent years suggests a path for our analysis, a bit of historical context on the topic of economic theory is useful before we dive into studying the details of the economy's broad swings. I begin with a recap of theory across the broad sweep of time. Where did the idea of analyzing the business cycle come from and how has it evolved?

In Chapter 2, I focus on the historical record of U.S. recessions and consider (briefly) some of the empirical efforts over the years that seek to put these events into perspective for anticipating the next round of contraction. If we're going to analyze recessions in detail, a primer on defining and profiling these events is a useful foundation.

For Chapters 3 through 11, the focus turns to studying each of the indicators that comprise the recession risk model that's presented at the end of the book. Yes, volumes could be (and have been) written about these indicators. But fear not, the goal here is merely a cursory introduction to the various data sets to provide a basic level of understanding for why these measures of economic and financial activity are on our short list.

Our journey concludes in Chapter 12 with a practical-minded review of a simple model for interpreting the various indicators that are discussed in the preceding chapters. I'll also point you to a free, publicly available business cycle index that can be used to compare and contrast with the book's model.

Yes, there are a lot of moving parts with analyzing recession risk. But after several years of study and trial-and-error analysis, I'm confident that I've developed a modest but powerful process for estimating macro danger. It's only natural—and intellectually healthy—that readers will be skeptical at this point. By the end of the book, however, I trust that quite a lot of the doubts will fade.

The true test of any system of economic evaluation is the one that unfolds in real time, and so only time can dispense the definitive conclusion. But as a preview, I've been running tests in recent years and the results are encouraging. For an ongoing update, visit my web site: CapitalSpectator.com, where I discuss strategic-minded economic and financial subjects—including the monthly signals dispensed by the model that's outlined in this book.[16]

Without further ado, let's begin… at the beginning, of course.

---

[16] See the author's web site (CapitalSpectator.com) and search for "US Economic Profile."

PART I

HISTORY IN PERSPECTIVE

Chapter 1

A Brief History Of Business Cycle Theory

From inference, intuition and divine inspiration
to dynamic stochastic general equilibrium (in only 30 centuries, give or take)

Analyzing the big picture in economics is an ancient art, but it's a relatively recent arrival as a formal field of study. The word "macroeconomics" doesn't even appear in the literature until the 1940s.[1] The origins, however, stretch back to the dawn of recorded history. You might say that the study of the business cycle is the oldest new idea in the dismal science.

One of the earliest efforts at applying a crude form of econometric modeling comes to us via the ancient Egyptians, who monitored the Nile's shifting water levels for clues about future harvests. Gathering crops constituted "a large part of what we would call their GDP," or gross domestic product, a modern measure of a nation's output.[2] Perhaps this Egyptian practice tells us why economic prophesy shows up in the Book of Genesis: "There will come seven years of great plenty throughout all the land of Egypt, but after them there will arise seven years of famine, and all the plenty will be forgotten in the land of Egypt....[3] Joseph's prediction sounds like a prototypical macro forecast. In any case, it's a hard act to follow for analysts lacking divine guidance. But ancient habits die hard, even if full clarity is still beyond the grasp of mortals. As the Book of Isaiah reminds: "Tell us what the future holds, so we may know that you are gods."[4]

There are no gods in the world of economic forecasting, but there's a long history of faulting higher powers for those times when chaos reigns, including economic troubles. The legal code of the Caesars carved out a recognition for *vis maior*, or superior force. The Roman Empire eventually crumbled, but the custom of formally blaming a deity in court survived. With the rise of Christendom in Europe, *vis maior* became *force majeure*, as it's known in French. The concept evolved into the "Act of God" reference, which describes various forms of blowback that's unleashed by war, Mother Nature, and other debacles beyond our control. Unsurprisingly, recessions eventually were added to this infamous list once the industrial revolution was underway and the modern business cycle became a recurring threat.

As the age of commercial enterprise was stirring, the legal groundwork was being laid for the rise of the Act of God defense. In the 16th century, English courts were turning the water of Roman legal precedent into modernity's civic wine. The precise origins in English law for this line of argument are lost to history, although the legendary *Shelley's Case* of 1581 determined that "it would be unreasonable that those things which are inevitable by the Act of God, which no industry can avoid, nor policy prevent should be construed to the prejudice of any person in whom there

---

[1] Mankiw (2006), p. 30.
[2] Hawkins (2005), p. 2. He cites discussions of early forecasters in Cox (1929) and Lebergott (1945).
[3] Genesis 41:29-30.
[4] Isaiah 41:21-23.

was no laches [negligence]."[5] In other words, sometimes an Act of God creates obstacles to enforcing contracts, and in those circumstances a defendant may not be responsible for any losses incurred.

This odd corner of legal precedent lives on in the modern age. The U.S. Congress, for instance, recently affirmed the concept's power and relevance by formally recognizing in federal regulations that an "'Act of God' means an unanticipated grave natural disaster or other natural phenomenon of an exceptional, inevitable, and irresistible character the effects of which could not have been prevented or avoided by the exercise of due care or foresight."[6]

Invoking the Act of God defense attracted new attention when the business cycle turned unusually ugly in the early 21st century. One of the more colorful examples in recent history arose in the waning days of 2008, at the height of the worst recession since the Great Depression. During that autumn of our collective discontent, the animated real estate magnate Donald Trump faced a problem not entirely of his own making. The final phase of his unfinished Chicago skyscraper was halted by a familiar but formidable obstacle: a shrinking economy.

In the wake of the financial crisis that engulfed Wall Street and ambushed the wider world that fall, sales fell precipitously for the unfinished Trump International Hotel and Tower in Chicago. As 2008 limped to its close, the economic carnage roaring through the U.S. became unmistakable and, for many, unbearable. Yet there was still the issue of the remaining loans on Trump's ledger, somewhere in excess of $300 million, including $40 million of construction debt that was personally guaranteed by the property czar. On November 6, 2008, he could take the pressure no more and "The Donald" filed suit against his lenders. He argued that a temporary reprieve was in order before he paid off his loans because of turmoil in the credit markets—turmoil that was triggered at least in part by a financial crisis and a deepening recession. Trump's legal argument was that *force majeure* intervened. A superior force—an Act of God—prevented him from paying off his debts in a timely manner.

"Would you consider the biggest depression we have had in this country since 1929 to be such an event?" Trump asked a reporter shortly after filing the claim. "I would," he replied, answering his own question. "A depression is not within the control of the borrower."[7]

Millions of homeowners also found themselves on the short end of the Great Recession in late-2008. But when confronted with the theoretical question of whether Trump would allow a buyer to back out of a contract that obligated the purchase of a Trump condominium at a higher pre-recession price, the tycoon summarily rejected the idea. "They don't have a *force majeure* clause," he reasoned.[8] Neither, it turned out, did Trump, after a court eventually ruled that he didn't have a deity to lean on.

---

[5] Wolfe v. Shelley, 76 Eng. Rep. 220 (1581). For a contemporary summary and analysis of the historical context, see Binder (1996).

[6] Oil Pollution Act, 33 USC § 2701 (1) (2006) and Comprehensive Environmental Response, Compensation, and Liability Act, 42 U.S.C. § 9601(1) (2006).

[7] Norris (2008).

[8] Ibid.

The Rise of the Quants

Looking down (at the numbers) rather than up (to God) for economic explanations of the broad trend began in earnest in the 17th century. William Petty, an English political economist, is credited with laying the foundation for modern econometric analytics. Taking inspiration from the scientific methods forged by Francis Bacon and Thomas Hobbes, Petty's empirical approach established a school of inquiry that marks the rudimentary start of economic research as we know it. As early as 1662, Petty wrote about the "Cycle" and how "Dearths and Plenties make their revolution" in commerce.[9]

In the following century, the formative stages of cycle theory blossomed as economists pushed deeper into a subject that would later be called macroeconomics. The French-Irish banker and speculator Richard Cantillon explored cause and effect between the money supply and economic trends in his only surviving work, *An Essay on Economic Theory*, which was probably written around 1730.[10] Aggregate spending "will always have completely different consequences than it seems to have for an individual" and "the first person to illustrate this theory in form of an economic cycle was Richard Cantillon," advised a recent history of economic theory.[11]

Francois Quesnay, the court physician to King Louis XV of France and one of Cantillon's contemporaries, developed an analytical description of economic activity in *Tableau économique* (Economic Table). This mid-18th century system profiled the cyclical flows of output and income by presuming a natural order that kept an economic system in equilibrium. "Tableau Economique illustrated how important money was to the economic cycle, even though this was not entirely clear to the physiocrats themselves at that time," observed economics professor Ulrich van Suntum in his textbook on economic history.[12]

If there was any debate in the mid-18th century about the connection between money and a nation's economy, David Hume attempted to clear away any confusion by outlining what he considered to be the final word on the subject. The Scottish philosopher, historian and economist argued that the rise and fall of liquidity was an explicit driver of the commercial cycle. In his succinct 1752 treatise "Of Money," Hume analyzed the relationship between prices and inflation, effectively describing what would evolve into a monetary based quantity theory of money:

> In my opinion, it is only in this interval or intermediate situation, between the acquisition of money and rise of prices, that the encreasing quantity of gold and silver is favourable to industry. When any quantity of money is imported into a nation, it is not at first dispersed into many hands; but is confined to the coffers of a few persons, who immediately seek to employ it to advantage... They are thereby enabled to employ more workmen than formerly, who never dream of demanding higher wages, but are glad of employment from such good paymasters. If workmen become scarce, the manufacturer gives higher wages, but at first requires an encrease of labour... The farmer and gardener, finding, that all their

---

[9] Petty ([1662] 1899), p. 43.
[10] Cantillon ([1755] 2010). Thorton (2006) provides a good summary of Cantillon's contributions to business cycle theory.
[11] van Suntum (2005), p. 80.
[12] Ibid., p. 82.

commodities are taken off, apply themselves with alacrity to the raising more; and at the same time can afford to take better and more cloths from their tradesmen, whose price is the same as formerly, and their industry only whetted by so much new gain. It is easy to trace the money in its progress through the whole commonwealth; where we shall find, that it must first quicken the diligence of every individual, before it encrease the price of labour.[13]

Reflecting on this seminal essay in 2001, Harvard economist Greg Mankiw wrote that Hume's analysis of the supply of money, inflation and the labor market "is an amazing quotation" because "it shows that this basic lesson of business cycle theory has been understood for well over two centuries."[14]

Hume died in 1776, a year that also witnessed America's declaration of political independence and the publication of *The Wealth of Nations*, Adam Smith's grand opus. The book is considered by many as the founding document in modern economics. Among its enduring claims to fame is its now-classic rationale for laissez-faire, or the idea that minimal government interference is the best strategy for delivering optimal economic results. "It is not from the benevolence of the butcher, the brewer, or the baker, that we expect our dinner, but from their regard to their own interest," Smith wrote. "We address ourselves, not to their humanity but to their self-love, and never talk to them of our own necessities but of their advantages."[15]

Central to Smith's view is an assumption that a natural market equilibrium exists that promotes a self-correcting economy. Gluts and shortages in this worldview are expected to be short-lived episodes of imbalance. Smith wasn't blind to the troubles that can arise from monetary shocks, inflation and "over-trading."[16] But the so-called classical economists, of whom Smith remains the pre-eminent member, "were not primarily concerned with the adjustments of the economy to the growth process, but with how such a process could be generated and sustained," Thomas Sowell observed.[17]

It wasn't until the 19th century that the dark side of the economy's fluctuations attracted attention as a subject worthy of study in its own right. A fair amount of debate during the fertile evolution of macro theory in the 1800s was sparked by what's known as Say's Law, which can be reduced to the claim that supply creates its own demand. For every seller there is a buyer, according to this idea. The theory's

---

[13] Hume ([1752] 1987)

[14] Mankiw (2001), p. C46.

[15] Smith ([1776], 1981), pp. 26-27 (Vol. I).

[16] Ibid., pp. 437-438: "Sober men, whose projects have been disproportioned to their capitals, are as likely to have neither wherewithal to buy money nor credit to borrow it, as prodigals whose expence has been disproportioned to their revenue. Before their projects can be brought to bear, their stock is gone, and their credit with it. They run about every-where to borrow money, and everybody tells them that they have none to lend. Even such general complaints of the scarcity of money do not always prove that the usual number of gold and silver pieces are not circulating in the country, but that many people want those pieces who have nothing to give for them. When the profits of trade happen to be greater than ordinary, over-trading becomes a general error both among great and small dealers."

[17] Sowell (1974), p. 33.

genesis is attributed to Jean-Baptiste Say, who, in his 1803 book *A Treatise on Political Economy*, counseled that "we must never lose sight of this maxim, that products are always bought ultimately with products"[18] and "the glut of a particular commodity arises from its having outrun the total demand for it in one or two ways; either because it has been produced in excessive abundance, or because the production of other commodities has fallen short."[19]

Few concepts are more contentious in economics than Say's Law, although the underlying reasoning is quite sensible in the context of the long run. As a simple example, imagine an economy with only two goods: bricks and glass. The brick maker can purchase glass with money earned from selling bricks; alternatively, he can engage in a barter transaction with the glassmaker, exchanging one commodity for the other. Either way, supply generates demand—albeit with a critical stipulation:

The laws of economics that apply in the long run don't always hold in the short term, a point that wasn't fully understood in the 19th century, when Say's Law was widely accepted as orthodoxy. But at least one dismal scientist of the era begged to differ: Jean Sismondi, "a neglected pioneer," as Sowell labeled him.[20] Sismondi's analysis of the rise and fall of a nation's short-term economic fortunes was an empirical attack on the claim that equilibrium prevails, as explained by the leading economists of the day, including David Ricardo. Sismondi didn't accept the consensus view, nor was he shy about announcing his dissent to the wider world. "Let us beware of this dangerous theory of equilibrium which is supposed to be automatically established," he warned in his 1819 book *New Principles of Political Economy*. "A certain kind of equilibrium, it is true, is reestablished in the long run, but it is only after a frightful amount of suffering."[21]

Sismondi wasn't a socialist, but his writings foreshadowed ideas that would find favor in the collectivist movement later in the century. Karl Marx recognized the value of Sismondi's analysis as ammunition for the socialist cause and wrote in 1863 that "Sismondi is profoundly conscious of the contradictions in capitalist production.... Hence, according to Sismondi, crises are not accidental, as Ricardo maintains, but essential outbreaks—occurring on a large scale and at definite periods—of the immanent contradictions."[22]

But Sismondi didn't go far enough for Marx, the "angry genius," as the economic historian Robert Heilbroner labeled him.[23] Marx threw the baby out with the bath water and indicted capitalism writ large as the primary source of economic volatility.

---

[18] Say ([1803], 1855), p. 161. The phrase supply creates its own demand has been attributed to the 20th century economist John Maynard Keynes, who wrote: "... supply creates its own demand in the sense that the aggregate demand price is equal to the aggregate supply price for all levels of output and employment" (Keynes ([1936] 1964), p. 21)). Yet some scholars advise that the primary source for the rephrasing of Say's text into its popular form is James Mill (John Stuart Mill's father), who wrote shortly after Say's book was published: "The production of commodities creates, and is the one and universal cause which creates a market for the commodities produced" (Mill (1808), p. 81).

[19] Ibid., p. 135.

[20] Sowell (1972).

[21] *New Principles (Nouveauax Principes)*, Vol. I, pp. 220-221, quoted in Newman (1952), pp. 143-144.

[22] Marx ([1863] 1969), p. 55.

[23] Heilbroner ([1953] 1986), p. 139.

In the process, he dismissed Say's Law as "childish... dogma."[24] Overproduction was endemic to capitalism, Marx argued in his masterwork, *Capital*, and so by his reasoning it followed that crises were an inevitable byproduct of the system.

To be fair, the classical economists also recognized the risk of general gluts—recessions. They did, however, dispute the source of these periodic downturns. Inadequate demand isn't the problem, they explained; rather, the culprit is excess supply. "Mistakes may be made, and commodities not suited to the demand may be produced—of these there may be a glut," Ricardo wrote.[25]

Thomas Malthus, who sparred with Ricardo for years, famously disagreed. Rejecting the classical view, Malthus saw gluts as the byproduct of underconsumption (weak demand).[26] Ricardo argued otherwise, writing to Malthus in 1820 that "Men err in their productions, [but] there is no deficiency of demand."[27] Ricardo's view wasn't universally accepted in his day, but the rising influence of his perspective in the decades after his death in 1823 became unmistakable. For example, John Stuart Mill's *Principles of Political Economy* in 1848 restated Ricardo's theory by arguing that "production is not excessive but merely ill-assorted" during economic slumps[28] because "all sellers are inevitably... buyers."[29]

Denying the possibility that demand failure could trigger a glut left the classically influenced economists with limited wiggle room by the latter half of the 19th century. It was increasingly obvious in the post-Civil War period that recessions were a routine part of the macroeconomic landscape in the rapidly industrializing economies of the U.S. and Europe. Yet this empirical fact didn't jibe with the models inspired by Say and Ricardo, leaving the defenders of the faith with an awkward question: How could theorists account for booms and busts without abandoning Say's Law?

One approach is to blame exogenous events—bolts from the blue that temporarily throw the system off balance. One of the more creative efforts on this front was devised by William Stanley Jevons, who looked beyond this world—literally—and claimed that the economy's earthly fluctuations are linked with the cycles of solar activity.[30]

Leon Walrus, a French economist who's credited with quantifying the theory of equilibrium in economics in the late-19th century, also recognized the occasional bouts of disequilibrium. Despite his mastery of mathematical economics, Walrus struggled to explain the phenomenon of gluts. "Such is the continuous market, which is perpetually tending towards equilibrium without ever actually attaining it," Walrus wrote in *Elements of Pure Economics*, "because

---

[24] Marx ([1867] 1915), p. 127.

[25] Ricardo (2005), Vol. 2, p. 305.

[26] See Malthus (1836), Book II, Chapter I, Section X, esp. pp. 414-420.

[27] Ricardo (2005), Vol. 8, p. 277.

[28] Mill ([1848] 1909), p. 559.

[29] Ibid., p. 558.

[30] Jevons (1875). Decades after Jevons advanced his sun-spot theory, another economist gazed skyward in search of solutions to macroeconomic riddles on terra firma: Henry Ludwell Moore in the 1920s found a causal link between the movement of the planet Venus and the business cycle.

the market has no other way of approaching equilibrium except by groping, and, before the goal is reached, it has to renew its efforts and start over again, all the basic data of the problem, e.g. the initial quantities possessed, the utilities of goods and services, the technical coefficients, the excess of income over consumption, the working capital requirements, etc. having changed in the meantime.... For, just as a lake is, at times, stirred to its very depths by a storm, so also the market is sometimes thrown into violent confusion by crises, which are sudden and general disturbances of equilibrium.[31]

Walrus conceded that "equilibrium in production, like equilibrium in exchange, is an ideal and not a real state." But he still argued that "equilibrium is the normal state, in the sense that it is the state towards which things spontaneously tend under a regime of free competition in exchange and in production."[32]

A few years later, Alfred Marshall—the influential British economist at Cambridge who dominated the field from the late-1800s until his death in 1924—acknowledged the recurrence of commercial crises. But he dismissed the idea that it was due to excess production (supply). In *The Economics of Industry*, which Marshall co-wrote with his wife (who was also an economist), the start of a crisis is described as "really nothing but a state of commercial disorganization; and that the remedy is a revival of confidence." The husband-and-wife team explained that "though men have the power to purchase they may not choose to use it. For when confidence has been shaken by failures, capital cannot be got to start new companies or extend news ones."[33]

Cycles, Not Crises
The appreciation that periodic crises could play havoc with the economic landscape attracted considerable attention in the latter half of the 19th century. Some economists began to rethink the view that occasional episodes of instability could be marginalized as isolated events that are unworthy of serious study. Instead, a few intrepid minds considered the disruptions to equilibrium as part of an ongoing systematic process, as opposed to seeing these events as solitary and unconnected upheavals. An early advocate of this notion was Clement Juglar, a Parisian doctor and economist. His 1862 book *Commercial Crises and Their Periodic Return* is considered a crucial link in the transition from theories of crises to proper business cycle models.

Joseph Schumpeter, among the early 20th century's leading economic theorists, opined in a 1931 lecture that Juglar "made the discovery that what the former generations had called 'crises' were no disconnected events, but merely elements in a more deep-seated wave-like movement. The crises are nothing but turning points from prosperity into depression, and it is the alternation between prosperity and depression which is the really interesting phenomenon."[34]

---

[31] Walras, Leon, ([1874] 1954), pp. 380-381.

[32] Ibid., p. 224

[33] Marshall and Marshall (1879), p. 154.

[34] Cited in Dal-Pont Legrand and Hagemann (2007), p. 2. Schumpeter's lecture, delivered at the Imperial University of Tokyo, was published in English in a Japanese economic journal as "The Theory of the Business Cycle," *Keizaigaku Ronshu – Journal of Economics* (April

Juglar and like-minded economists also laid the groundwork for the empirical econometric approach that would bloom in the early years of the 20th century, largely under the early guidance of Wesley Clair Mitchell. In his 1913 book *Business Cycles and Their Causes*, Mitchell defined what is still the empiricist's credo for analyzing the business cycle:

> There is slight hope of getting answers to these questions by a logical process of proving and criticizing the theories. For whatever merits of ingenuity and consistency they may possess, these theories have slight value except as they give keener insight into the phenomena of business cycles. It is by study of the facts which they purport to interpret that the theories must be tested.[35]

For Mitchell, the path was clear: "To observe, analyze, and systematize the phenomena of prosperity, crisis, and depression is the chief task," he wrote. Theory, although useful for guidance, threatened to distract analysts from the primary goal. "There is better prospect of rendering service if we attack this task directly," he reasoned, "than if we take the round-about way of considering the phenomena with reference to the theories."[36] Mitchell didn't dismiss theory, but he made a conscious effort to focus on the data. As Milton Friedman observed years later, "Mitchell is generally considered primarily an empirical scientist rather than a theorist."[37]

Mitchell's rise as an influential researcher and analyst on matters of the business cycle eventually created a fair degree of tension vis-à-vis the theoretical school of economics. Tjalling Koopmans, in a widely cited and critical review of a book that Mitchell co-wrote with Arthur Burns, labeled the empirical methodology as "measurement without theory."[38] From the theorists' point of view, the Mitchells of the world were searching for solutions without context or substance—blindly grasping for answers without knowing where to look, Koopmans argued. Only theory could provide the necessary perspective and foundation to tell us which variables are important for assessing the business cycle, and which ones are useless or misleading.

The criticism still resonates in the 21st century in debates about the value of econometric analysis for describing and understanding the business cycle. But time and evolving techniques have mellowed the arguments and each side has moved closer to the other through the decades, albeit in parallel universes.

As for Mitchell, he went on to found the National Bureau of Economic Research, which became and remains the official arbiter of the U.S. business cycle dates. Considering this organization's history, it's no surprise that NBER decisions on the

---

1931). The lecture is also available at: www.schumpeter.info/text2~1.htm. Note, however, that Besomi (2010) emphasized that Schumpeter oversimplified Juglar's historical role as a leading founder of business cycle theory. Rather, Juglar was one of many intellectuals responsible for the transition from crisis theory to business cycle theory in the mid-19th century, according to Besomi.

[35] Mitchell (1913), p. 19.
[36] Ibid., p. 20.
[37] Sherman (2001), p. 85.
[38] Koopmans (1947), p. 161.

start and end of the economy's major trends still lean heavily on observation and subjective interpretation rather than theory.

Meanwhile, the empiricists continue to defend their case, in part by emphasizing that it's never clear when, or if, theory is superior for explaining or forecasting economic activity. No one really knows what's relevant for deconstructing the broad fluctuations in a nation's output. In turn, the intellectual limitations cast doubts about the value of a given theory. The challenge is further complicated by the existence of theories that sometimes conflict with one another. No wonder that deciding what works and what doesn't in economic forecasting continues to rely on trial and error and letting the numbers suggest what's important, or not.

Business cycle theory, in any case, continued to evolve after Mitchell published his 1913 book. In fact, the years between the world wars of the 20th century were as ambitious and productive as any in macroeconomic history, before or since. If there was common ground among the theorists and the empiricists, it was the general agreement that a cycle persists. The theorists, however, were more concerned with figuring out why it persists, as opposed to the empiricists' somewhat more practical goal of anticipating the major turning points.

For some economists, the solution to deciphering why there was a business cycle in the first place was closely linked to analyzing the private sector's poor choices in the deployment of capital. British economist Arthur Pigou, for example, revived Marshall's point that confidence (or the lack thereof) about the future is a crucial factor for developing a viable theory. "The varying expectations of business men... constitute the immediate cause and direct causes or antecedents of industrial fluctuations," he advised in his 1927 book *Industrial Fluctuations*.[39]

A reasonable assumption, perhaps, but in a world where forecasting is problematic and mistakes are inevitable, formal predictions don't easily stand the test of time. Pigou's contemporary, Friedrich Hayek, was keen on seeing the blunders by business leaders and policymakers as the foundation for trouble. He argued that carelessly loose monetary policy begets ill-conceived investments. The resulting mistakes with capital deployment have an annoying habit of leading an economy astray, Hayek warned. "Monetary policy is much more likely to be a cause rather than a cure of depressions," he asserted in his 1931 book *Prices and Production*. Hayek's solution: let the natural order of fluctuating supply and demand steer monetary policy. Years later, he wrote that "the past instability of the market economy is the consequence of the exclusion of the most important regulator of the market mechanism, money, from itself being regulated by the market process."[40]

Irving Fisher decided in 1933 that the notion of a business cycle as "a single, simple, self-generating cycle (analogous to that of a pendulum swinging under influence of the single force of gravity) and as actually realized historically in regularly recurring crises, is a myth. Instead of one force there are many forces."[41] He argued that "as explanations of the so-called business cycle, or cycles, when these are really serious, I doubt the adequacy of overproduction, under-consumption, over-capacity, price-dislocation, maladjustment between agricultural and industrial

---

[39] Pigou (1927), p. 29.
[40] Hayek (1999), p. 202.
[41] Fisher (1933), p. 338.

prices, over-confidence, over-investment, over-saving, over-spending, and the discrepancy between saving and investment."[42]

Debt and deflation, on the other hand, "are, in the great booms and depressions, more important causes than all others put together," Fisher claimed. Writing during the depths of Great Depression, he became convinced "that if debt and deflation are absent, other disturbances are powerless to bring on crises comparable in severity to those of 1837, 1873, or 1929-33."[43] No wonder that monetary policy is crucial in Fisher's understanding of economic volatility. Recognizing a central bank's ability to influence, if not dictate, inflation, deflation, and the demand for money is essential for deciphering the business cycle in a Fisherian worldview.

John Maynard Keynes was somewhat sympathetic to this explanation, but sometimes economic problems arise because of the meandering and imprudent perceptions that bedevil the human condition, he warned in *The General Theory of Employment, Interest, and Money*, his famous 1936 book that's widely credited with formalizing the field of macroeconomics. Changes in sentiment, or "animal spirits"—the "spontaneous urge to action rather than inaction"—can bring a sharp but not always explicable tumble in an economy's aggregate demand when the crowd turns pessimistic, Keynes wrote.[44]

In fact, aggregate demand is the key to understanding recessions generally, and the Great Depression specifically, according to Keynes. When demand slides across an economy, for whatever reason, a nation's output and income soon follow. The result: higher unemployment, otherwise known as a recession. Waiting for the economy to right itself and return to equilibrium is risky, according to this school of thought—particularly when a drop in aggregate demand is unusually steep. Government intervention, as a result, should play a critical role in stabilizing the economy during these events.

At the heart of Keynes' analysis is what's known as the paradox of thrift. Although it's rational for an individual to save more and spend less in times of hardship, the economy suffers when everyone is thrifty. The result, according to Keynes, is that aggregate demand falls as overall savings rise. The solution, he argued, is a temporary program of additional government spending to make up for the private sector's shrunken demand.

Rethinking Orthodoxy
After World War II, Keynesian thinking dominated macroeconomic theory and practice for a generation. A pillar of support was the widespread belief that economic growth generally, and low unemployment specifically, could be promoted and sustained by engineering higher inflation. But by the late-1960s, the models inspired by *The General Theory* attracted a new wave of criticism. There were several catalysts behind the growing discontent with Keynesian, although the main source of doubt was triggered by the arrival of stagflation, or the combination of elevated inflation and sluggish economic growth.

"In the late 1960s and early 1970s, there were strains on the U.S. economy caused by the cost of President Johnson's War on Poverty and the simultaneous escalation

---

[42] Ibid., p. 340.
[43] Ibid., p. 341.
[44] Keynes ([1936] 1964), p. 161.

of the Vietnam War at a time when the economy had already been brought to near-full employment by the successful application of Keynesian fiscal policy," according to economist Roger Backhouse. "As a result, the inflation rate began to rise."[45] When the economy was expanding, higher inflation was tolerable if not ignored. But the tolerance quickly evaporated after Egypt and Syria launched a war on Israel in October 1973—an attack that instigated an Arab oil embargo that drove energy prices to unprecedented heights. The resulting macro shock of soaring energy prices threw the oil-dependent U.S. economy into a tailspin. But this time the shock also stoked inflation.

The combination of recession and high inflation was unusual, although the dual-edged problem wasn't entirely unexpected. As early as 1945, Harvard economist Gottfried Haberler warned that success with government-based stimulus policies intent on juicing the economy was far from certain. One of his concerns was the risk that policy prescriptions would be "overdone" and lead to what would later be called stagflation:

> There may be a large volume of unemployment that cannot be cured by increasing general expenditure. If the unemployed are concentrated in certain "depressed" areas and industries, while there is full employment elsewhere, a general increase in expenditure would only serve to drive up prices in the full employment area, without having much effect on the depressed industries. Then the paradox of depression and unemployment in midst of inflation would be experienced.[46]

A real world run of something approximating the "paradox of depression and unemployment in the midst of inflation" arrived several decades later. The stagflation of the 1970s presented new challenges for Keynesian economics. Hanging in the balance: the relevance of the Phillips curve, otherwise known as the tradeoff between inflation and the jobless rate.

The idea that higher inflation is linked with lower unemployment, and vice versa, claims a long pedigree in economics. The modern formulation dates to a 1958 study by economist William Phillips, who profiled an inverse relationship between changes in wages and unemployment in the United Kingdom.[47] The Phillips curve offered what also appeared to be a reasonable description of U.S. economic activity in the post-war era. But the relationship seemed to crack under the macro pressures of the 1970s.

The fallout from stagflation didn't exactly shock Keynesian economists, who always recognized that prices are "sticky," particularly for wages. In other words, prices don't fall as fast as unemployment rises, which may explain why an economy doesn't transition to equilibrium quickly after a recession strikes. But if this was old news in Keynesian circles, the critics smelled blood amid the economic chaos of the

---

[45] Backhouse (2010), p. 127.

[46] Haberler (1945), p. 107. For some political-historical background on the rise of Keynesian policies in the post-war U.S. economy, see Wapshott (2011), chapter 15, which led me to Haberler's paper.

[47] Phillips (1958). Although the relationship between inflation and unemployment is widely attributed as a discovery by Phillips, Irving Fisher wrote about the phenomenon in 1926 (see Fisher ([1926] 1973)).

1970s. Unfairly or not, there was a growing perception that Keynesian had failed, opening the door for the embrace of new explanations of the business cycle.

Among the beneficiaries was monetarism. Rumblings of an assault on Keynesian orthodoxy had been bubbling for years, including Milton Friedman's argument that the money supply is the critical variable, as he asserted in his 1956 paper "The Quantity Theory of Money: A restatement." Echoing what Hume had written 200 years earlier, Friedman revitalized and modernized the argument that fluctuations in the amount of money circulating was the leading factor behind macro volatility. The idea was fleshed out in greater detail in his magnum opus, which he co-authored with Anna Schwartz: *A Monetary History of the United States, 1861-1960*. Published in 1963, the book reviewed U.S. economic history, in part, through the lens of the money supply. One of its legacies is the shifting of blame for the Great Depression from capitalism and free markets to the Federal Reserve's errors in the management of monetary policy in the early 1930s. Friedman and Schwartz, drawing on a battery of statistics, argued that the central bank failed to provide sufficient liquidity in a timely manner to satisfy the sharp and sudden rise in money demand—an oversight that allowed deflation to infect the economy, the authors charged.

In 1967, Friedman attacked Keynesian by way of the Phillips curve, arguing in a famous speech to the American Economic Association that the jobless rate couldn't be kept low by tolerating relatively high inflation. The problem, he explained, is that

> ...there is always a temporary trade-off between inflation and employment; [but] there is no permanent trade-off. The temporary trade-off comes not from inflation per se, but from unanticipated inflation, which generally means, from a rising rate of inflation. The widespread belief that there is a permanent trade-off is a sophisticated version of the confusion between "high" and "rising" that we all recognize in simpler forms. A rising rate of inflation may reduce unemployment, a high rate will not.[48]

The issue here is the expectation that elevating economic output above its potential, or equilibrium, rate would eventually backfire as workers became accustomed to an environment of higher inflation. They would soon ask for higher inflation-adjusted wages as compensation. The arrival of stagflation a few years after Friedman delivered his speech seemed to confirm the warning.

If Friedman represented the forefront of the empirical wing of the attack on Keynesianism, his counterpart on the theoretical side of the aisle was Robert Lucas, who was teaching at Carnegie Mellon University when he launched his intellectual strike on the status quo. In a series of papers in 1970s, he challenged Keynesian economics with what would become known as rational expectations models, from which evolved the real business cycle theory (RBCT). The foundation of Lucas' charge is that Keynesian analysis and its prescriptions were built on shaky economics. As a remedy, Lucas and like-minded dismal scientists developed models

---

[48] Friedman (1968), p. 11. In a paper published the same year that Friedman gave his speech, Edmund Phelps independently established that there was no long-run tradeoff between inflation and unemployment: (Phelps (1967)).

that were said to be more rigorous than their Keynesian counterparts—new classical economics, as some dubbed it.

In a 1993 interview, Lucas explained how he came to oppose the Keynesian view, asserting that

> ...no one ever thought Keynesian economics was good economics. From the start, at least in the United States, there was an effort to unify Keynesian economics with neoclassical economics. Paul Samuelson really started that, or maybe Franco Modigliani. So even Keynesians were unhappy with Keynesian economics. There was an effort that everyone was engaged in to provide a microeconomic foundation for Keynesian models. Thinking that was a desirable thing to do was not the same as opposing Keynesian economics. Everyone believed in it.
>
> It just seems that as we got further and further toward finding something that looked like it might be a microeconomic foundation, it got less and less Keynesian. Finally some of us decided it wasn't Keynesian at all, and that was that.[49]

The RBCT, for all its influence as an alternative to Keynesian theory, is built on several principles that conflict with conventional (some might say naïve) thinking about how an economy operates. For example, RBCT rejects the traditional view that the business cycle is a process of periodic fluctuations. The appearance of a cycle, in other words, is an illusion. Instead, an economy's ups and downs are driven by random, unpredictable shocks. According to RBCT, only "real" shocks matter, as opposed to "nominal" shocks, such as changes in monetary policy. Real shocks are responsible for what appears to the untrained eye as a series of cyclical booms and busts. An unexpected surge in oil prices or a new set of regulations, for instance, are real shocks that can alter productivity levels, which affects growth and encourages consumers and businesses to adjust spending, investment, and savings. The message here is that analyzing so-called patterns in historical data is deeply flawed in the quest to anticipate the future.

Some RBCT explanations led to surprising and controversial narratives. Perhaps the starkest example is a comparison of RBCT with the orthodoxy of Keynesian for explaining the rise of unemployment during recessions. According to the Keynesian view, workers lose their jobs through no fault of their own; rather, the newly unemployed are victims of a general decline in aggregate demand—a recession. In that case, the solution is reviving demand. Since aggregate demand shortfalls are directly linked to the private sector, the government should temporarily step in to keep the economy in equilibrium.

RBCT doesn't see it this way. Instead, unemployment is a function of workers making poor decisions because they have limited information about prices. A highly paid executive who loses her job, for instance, chooses to remain jobless rather than take a lower-paying position with the Micawber-like expectation that something better will turn up. In short, unemployment is modeled as a function of voluntary choices in RBCT's worldview of macro.

---

[49] Levy (1993).

Faulty decisions born of incomplete information lead to output fluctuations and disequilibrium in the economy, according to real business cycle theorists. Lucas added the money factor to the concept in a 1972 paper, which explained variations in unemployment as a consequence of the unpredictable aspect of monetary policy.[50] In 1976, Lucas went a step further and mounted a deeper challenge to Keynesian orthodoxy with the so-called Lucas critique, which warned that it's naïve to forecast economic changes based solely on the historical record.[51] He argued that the seemingly fixed structural relationships that govern the connections between macro variables—unemployment and inflation, for instance—can be highly dependent on the prevailing economic policy of the moment and the expectations that arise from transient programs and choices. As policies change, so too will expectations. The practical result is that standard econometric models that draw lessons from history may not work in the future, a point that resonated in the 1970s, when the historical relation between inflation and unemployment "disappeared."[52]

The prescription for avoiding the pitfalls of the Lucas critique is two-fold: identify the so-called deep structural parameters that explain the true nature of the business cycle; and model how consumers, businesses, and investors collectively react to policy changes. Many analysts over the years have taken the Lucas critique to heart and searched for those deep parameters. The results, however, are mixed at best, in part because it's devilishly difficult to identify the true parameters that govern the economy.[53]

Another problem is that the Lucas critique itself "is a testable empirical hypothesis."[54] The glitch leaves analysts with a choice that may be impossible to resolve. To be precise, it's unclear if focusing on the deep structural parameters that govern the economy will lead to better forecasts compared with using conventional econometric analyses. Sizing up the deep parameters is complicated and subject to all the usual pitfalls that come with making decisions about the broad economy. One study of RBCT's forecasting ability claimed that the theory's problematic because "it is unable to account for many features of the forecastable movements in output, consumption, and hours [worked]."[55]

But there's plenty of disagreement to go around. One analyst in 2001 countered that earlier tests that rejected RBCT were misleading due to oversimplification. As a result, RBCT models still have "the potential for making good forecasts" if you know how to use them properly.[56]

Revolutionary Blowback

Whatever the limits of the Lucas-inspired revolution, there's no denying its influence on macroeconomics and the challenges it presented for Keynesian models. Real business cycle theorists tend to see efforts at smoothing the business cycle—demand

---

[50] Lucas (1972).
[51] Lucas (1976).
[52] Atkeson and Ohanian (2001), p. 4.
[53] See Summers (1986) for an influential critique of real business cycle theory's limitations as a practical model.
[54] Estrella and Fuhrer (2003), p. 94.
[55] Rotemberg and Woodford (1996), pp. 71-72.
[56] Zimmermann (2001), p. 189.

management, as some call it—as irrelevant at best, and perhaps even damaging to the point of deepening recessions and restraining the recoveries. As Lucas wrote in 2009, the efficiency of the market teaches "the futility of trying to deal with crises and recessions by finding central bankers and regulators who can identify and puncture bubbles."[57] A controversial argument these days, but influential nonetheless.[58]

But just when it looked like the war over Keynesian theory had been won, events conspired to challenge the new status quo. After the turmoil of 2008, a fresh round of debate questioned the progress, if any, in macroeconomics for anticipating the future by way of so-called new and improved models. As one critic noted in the wake of the Great Recession:

> Now it is "dynamic stochastic general equilibrium" (DSGE) models inspired by the Lucas critique that have failed to predict or even explain the Great Recession of 2007–2009. More precisely, the implicit "explanations" based on these models are that the recession, including the millions of net jobs lost, was primarily due to large negative shocks to both technology and willingness to work.[59]

For many economists, the worst recession since the Great Depression of the 1930s called into question the value of the Lucas revolution. New classical economics became controversial all over again in the 21st century. For all its influence in the preceding decades, it's fair to say that it was never fully accepted, even in its pre-crisis heyday. Yes, the static models inspired by conventional Keynesian thinking were swept aside for a time by the embrace of the real expectations school, a shift that Lucas wasn't shy in promoting. But if this was supposed to lead to clearer forecasts and a deeper understanding of the cycle, the new classical adherents have a lot of explaining to do.

Critics of Lucas and company have been merciless in the post-2008 era, none more so than Paul Krugman, a Nobel-prizing-winning Keynesian economist at Princeton who hammered away at the rational expectations crowd as a *New York Times* columnist and blogger. In 2009, for instance, Krugman attacked the new classical movement by asking: "How did economists get it so wrong?"[60] The answer, or most of it, according to Krugman, is "the profession's blindness to the very possibility of catastrophic failures in a market economy." He concluded that "Keynesian economics remains the best framework we have for making sense of recessions and depressions." [61]

Only a few years earlier, Lucas emphasized the progress in the dismal science, as he saw it. "Macroeconomics... has succeeded," he asserted in a 2003 address to the American Economic Association. "Its central problem of depression prevention has been solved, for all practical purposes, and has in fact been solved for many

---

[57] Lucas (2009).
[58] For a good summary of the controversy and debate on macro theory, see "The other-worldly philosophers," *The Economist*, July 16, 2009.
[59] Morley (2010), p. 2.
[60] Krugman (2009).
[61] Ibid.

decades." In a dig at Keynesian economic policies, he added that "the potential for welfare gains from better long-run, supply-side policies exceeds by far the potential from further improvements in short-run demand management."[62]

The near-collapse of the financial system and the devastating recession of 2008-2009 have raised serious doubts about such claims, but the rational expectations crowd hasn't surrendered. Consider the recent views of Thomas Sargent, who shared the 2011 Nobel Prize in economics for his work on rational expectations models that emphasize an econometric framework for explaining how people adapt to changing economic conditions. Interviewed a year before he received the prize, he was asked to defend his branch of macro in the wake of the 2008-2009 economic crisis. He responded:

> The criticism of real business cycle models and their close cousins, the so-called New Keynesian models, is misdirected and reflects a misunderstanding of the purpose for which those models were devised.[63] These models were designed to describe aggregate economic fluctuations during normal times when markets can bring borrowers and lenders together in orderly ways, not during financial crises and market breakdowns.[64]

Lucas said something similar in 2009, warning that "one thing we are not going to have, now or ever, is a set of models that forecasts sudden falls in the value of financial assets, like the declines that followed the failure of Lehman Brothers in September [2008]." In fact, "this is nothing new," he explained:

> It has been known for more than 40 years and is one of the main implications of Eugene Fama's "efficient-market hypothesis" (EMH), which states that the price of a financial asset reflects all relevant, generally available information. If an economist had a formula that could reliably forecast crises a week in advance, say, then that formula would become part of generally available information and prices would fall a week earlier.[65]

Nonetheless, the critics insisted that the ideas of Lucas, Sargent and others are flawed if not dangerous. There are times, after all, when economic conditions aren't "normal." Economic models that offer little or no traction for periods of abnormality—recessions—have limited practical value in a world where economic slumps are a recurring menace. It's one thing to argue in an academic setting that the

---

[62] Lucas (2003), p. 1.

[63] The interviewer writes in a footnote here: "'New Keynesian economics' refers to the school of thought that has refined Keynes' original theories in response to the Lucas critique and rational expectations. Advocates of New Keynesian theory rely on the idea that prices and wages change slowly (referred to as "sticky" prices and wages) to explain why unemployment persists and why monetary policy can influence economic activity. But their models are adapted from the dynamic general equilibrium models developed by new classical economists such as Sargent and Lucas. See: www.econlib.org/library/Enc/NewKeynesianEconomics.html for elaboration."

[64] Rolnick (2010).

[65] Lucas (2009).

economy clears in the long run and so supply matches demand eventually. It's quite another matter to live through a recession in real time, particularly a deep and long-lasting one that incurs deep financial costs and shakes entire nations to their core.

Willem Buiter, chief economist of Citigroup, complained in 2009 that "most mainstream macroeconomic theoretical innovations since the 1970s… have turned out to be self-referential, inward-looking distractions at best." As a result, he charged, "the economics profession was caught unprepared when the crisis struck.[66]

It's (Still) All About The Numbers
Stepping back and considering the recent arguments in the context of history suggests that the debates about the business cycle haven't advanced all that much from the days when Ricardo and Malthus traded arguments in hand-written letters. It seems that macro has come full circle in its intellectual travels (again) since economists first began probing its mysteries in earnest in the 1800s. Meantime, the business cycle is still with us and dismal scientists continue to argue over cause and effect.

We may be no closer to explaining the business cycle, but evaluating the related risk is still in high demand in the 21st century. In fact, it's plausible to argue that the lack of progress on the former is directly related to the greater appetite for the latter. The challenge is deciding how to intelligently analyze the signals for insight about recession risk while managing the hazard that uncertainty and false alarms can never be completely eliminated. It's a delicate balancing act, but it's a task that we can't neglect—especially if future recessions are likely to be deeper as a general rule, as some economists predict.[67]

If there's any chance of learning from the past, we'll have to study the historical record in some detail. Theory offers guideposts for thinking about how to proceed, but there's no alternative to diving into the data. The pages ahead will focus on the empirical record, which leaves us open to Koopmans' charge of "measurement without theory." But evaluating the past for clues about how to evaluate recession risk in real time future is the only game in town.

Practical necessity dictates that the hard work ahead will rely rather heavily on studying the numbers—analysis that's informed by theory, but without being a slave to it. As Milton Friedman counseled:

> …the relevant question to ask about the "assumptions" of a theory is not whether they are descriptively "realistic," for they never are, but whether they are sufficiently good approximations for the purpose in hand. And this question can be answered only by seeing whether the theory works, which means whether it yields sufficiently accurate predictions.[68]

Before we can effectively search for those approximations, we need to understand what we're dealing with. In this chapter we've been referring to

---

[66] Buiter (2009).

[67] Stock and Watson (2012), for instance, warn that the "slowdown in trend employment growth" driven by "demographic factors… imply that future recessions will be deeper, and will have slower recoveries, than historically has been the case." (p. 3).

[68] Friedman (1953), p. 15.

recessions from the grand perspective of theory. But these events have distinguishing characteristics on the ground—characteristics that deserve careful inspection for our mission of determining when the risk of new recession looks unusually threatening.

If we're trying to defeat a rival, or at least defend ourselves from attacks, ignorance about the adversary is always a liability, perhaps fatally so. As the ancient Chinese military strategist Sun Tzu counseled in the *Art of War*, Know your enemy. With that in mind, it's time meet (and study) our opponent in some detail.

Chapter 2

Would You Know A Recession If You Saw One?

Discovering the business cycle

Never underestimate the potential for economic volatility, Ed Prescott counseled in 1986 in an attempt to square his interpretation of the real business cycle theory (RBCT) with the economy's bumpy historical record. "Economic fluctuations are optimal responses to uncertainty in the rate of technological change," he decided.[1] Under the narrative of RBCT, these changes, or shocks, can take several forms, such as a surge in energy prices, the blowback from new regulations, or the economic fallout unleashed by a weather-related event or natural disaster. Whatever the cause, shocks alter expectations among corporations and individuals by shifting decisions on a range of issues, from production and hiring to investing and consumption. In other words, *real* changes affect the economy, as opposed to *nominal* changes, which are primarily affected by monetary policy.

Real changes aren't a sign of market failure, Prescott emphasized. The quantity supplied still equals the quantity demanded. The market continues to clear, even if the clearing takes places at dramatically different prices under substantially altered conditions. In any case, real business cycle theory anticipates economic fluctuations of 5% or more, he advised. In fact, it would be puzzling if the economy didn't bounce around by more than trivial amounts.

Prescott's observation sounds like a modern version of Say's Law. In addition, his analysis suggests there's nothing odd about the history of the U.S. economy's volatility. The United States has suffered through 33 "optimal responses"—a.k.a. recessions—from the mid-nineteenth century through the 2007-2009 contraction, according to the National Bureau of Economic Research (NBER). Should we think of these events as something other than market failures? Are recessions merely the normal adjustment process of a capitalist economy that encounters new information about equilibrium?

Many economists have their doubts. "Real business cycle models of the type urged on us by Prescott have nothing to do with the business cycle phenomena observed in the United States or other capitalist economies," Larry Summers wrote in a pointed and widely cited rebuttal to Prescott's paper. [2] Even if we ignore the thicket of theoretical debate, it should be obvious by now that recessions don't bend to easy explanations. The basic discussion of how an economy works certainly starts out on an agreeable plane, but it quickly deteriorates from there.

James Hamilton, a professor of economics at University of California, San Diego, cited what amounts to a broad consensus on factors that explain why economies expand: a rising population of workers, more equipment and facilities, and a steady stream of improved tools and techniques for boosting productivity. "These three factors—population, capital stock, and technology—are widely

---

[1] Prescott (1986), p. 21.
[2] Summers (1986), p. 24.

regarded as the main drivers of long-run growth."[3] If so, one might look to one of these factors for deciphering recessions. But it's not that easy, Hamilton reminds:

> In a recession, we do not lose population; rather, an ever-growing number of people report that they are unable to find jobs. Capital stock is not destroyed, but instead sits idle. And although the hypothesis that recessions may be caused by an exogenous decline in productivity has been popular with real business cycle theorists, many do not find that explanation compelling. Something other than these three factors seems to be governing the aggregate economic behavior during particular identifiable episodes.[4]

Whatever the underlying cause of recessions, the tenacity of these periodic funks to roll across history isn't in doubt. Of the 33 slumps recorded for the U.S. since the mid-1800s, the average lasted nearly 18 months. The shortest was a brief six-month affair in 1980; the longest lasted more than five years: a 65-month monster that terrorized the country through 1879 (see Table 2.1).[5]

The good news is that the expansions generally run far longer than the contractions. Since 1945, the average period of growth is roughly 58 months vs. 11 months for recessions in the post-war decades. Business cycles, in other words, are asymmetrical; fortunately, they're asymmetrical in favor of growth.

Casually looking at the historical record may suggest that expansions die of old age; if so, recession risk mechanically rises as growth rolls on. But a closer review casts serious doubt on this idea. For one thing, recessions sometimes strike soon after the end of the previous contraction. The extreme example: the 1981 recession began just 13 months after the preceding downturn ended in July 1980. At other times, the period between two recessions extends for years—a decade in the case of the interval of between the 1990-1991 and 2001 slumps.

Not surprisingly, formal studies find minimal evidence in support of the idea that a natural aging process afflicts economic expansions.[6] It's true, of course, that time is a factor, albeit in a crude way. Assuming that recessions endure, one can argue that the potential for a new downturn increases with each passing day. But that's a bit like saying that we're all destined for the cemetery—correct, although recognizing this fate doesn't diminish the case for ongoing medical research, the fruits of which can enhance our lives in the years before the Grim Reaper pays a visit. Similarly, there's no reason why the fate of the business cycle should prevent us from looking for superior tools and techniques that will improve our understanding of recession risk.

---

[3] Hamilton (2011), p. 1006.

[4] Ibid., pp. 1006-1007.

[5] Here and throughout the book I use the convention of dating the start of recessions in the month *after* the cyclical peak, as published by NBER. The end of recessions remains the NBER trough date. For example, NBER identifies December 2007 as the peak month, and so the recession formally starts in January 2008; the end of the recession is the trough month of June 2009. Be aware that this rule isn't universally applied and so some pundits equate the first month of a new recession with the cyclical peak.

[6] For example, see Diebold and Rudebusch (2001), pp. 3-5, for a skeptical overview of the evidence that the risk of contractions rises the longer an expansion rolls on.

Table 2.1					
BUSINESS CYCLE REFERENCE DATES		DURATION IN MONTHS			
Peak	Trough	Contraction	Expansion	Cycle	
Quarterly dates are in parentheses		*Peak to Trough*	*Previous Trough to this Peak*	*Trough from Previous Trough*	*Peak from Previous Peak*
	December 1854 (IV)	--	--	--	--
June 1857(II)	December 1858 (IV)	18	30	48	--
October 1860(III)	June 1861 (III)	8	22	30	40
April 1865(I)	December 1867 (I)	32	46	78	54
June 1869(II)	December 1870 (IV)	18	18	36	50
October 1873(III)	March 1879 (I)	65	34	99	52
March 1882(I)	May 1885 (II)	38	36	74	101
March 1887(II)	April 1888 (I)	13	22	35	60
July 1890(III)	May 1891 (II)	10	27	37	40
January 1893(I)	June 1894 (II)	17	20	37	30
December 1895(IV)	June 1897 (II)	18	18	36	35
June 1899(III)	December 1900 (IV)	18	24	42	42
September 1902(IV)	August 1904 (III)	23	21	44	39
May 1907(II)	June 1908 (II)	13	33	46	56
January 1910(I)	January 1912 (IV)	24	19	43	32
January 1913(I)	December 1914 (IV)	23	12	35	36
August 1918(III)	March 1919 (I)	7	44	51	67
January 1920(I)	July 1921 (III)	18	10	28	17
May 1923(II)	July 1924 (III)	14	22	36	40
October 1926(III)	November 1927 (IV)	13	27	40	41
August 1929(III)	March 1933 (I)	43	21	64	34
May 1937(II)	June 1938 (II)	13	50	63	93
February 1945(I)	October 1945 (IV)	8	80	88	93
November 1948(IV)	October 1949 (IV)	11	37	48	45
July 1953(II)	May 1954 (II)	10	45	55	56
August 1957(III)	April 1958 (II)	8	39	47	49
April 1960(II)	February 1961 (I)	10	24	34	32
December 1969(IV)	November 1970 (IV)	11	106	117	116
November 1973(IV)	March 1975 (I)	16	36	52	47
January 1980(I)	July 1980 (III)	6	58	64	74
July 1981(III)	November 1982 (IV)	16	12	28	18
July 1990(III)	March 1991(I)	8	92	100	108
March 2001(I)	November 2001 (IV)	8	120	128	128
December 2007 (IV)	June 2009 (II)	18	73	91	81
Average, all cycles:					
1854-2009 (33 cycles)		17.5	38.7	56.2	56.4*
1854-1919 (16 cycles)		21.6	26.6	48.2	48.9**
1919-1945 (6 cycles)		18.2	35	53.2	53
1945-2009 (11 cycles)		11.1	58.4	69.5	68.5

Source: NBER   * 32 cycles   ** 15 cycles

The arrival date and duration of the next recession are always in doubt, but every downturn is sure to be a costly affair. An International Monetary Fund study summarized the economic fallout of 122 downturns in 21 advanced countries from 1960 through 2007. As you'd expect, the impact wasn't trivial. Economic output on average fell 2.6% in the sample of countries reviewed. In "severe" recessions—the worst 25% of recession-related losses—the decline is generally more than twice as deep (Figure 2.1).[7]

Figure 2.1
Average changes for select econonmic indicators during recessions
for 122 advanced countries: 1960-2007

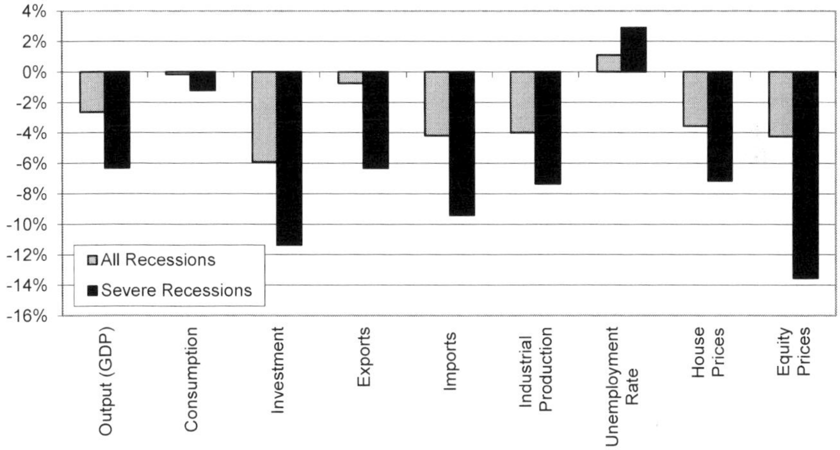

Source: Claessens, et al. (2008)

Before we go any further, now's a good time to recognize that the use of the word "cycle" is a misnomer. Yes, it's invoked throughout this book and it's commonly cited by analysts and the news media. But it's used primarily as a rhetorical convenience. The tradition of calling the economy's alternating phases of growth and contraction a business *cycle* may have been inspired by the pre-World War II experience, when fluctuations, according to one economic historian, were considered "fairly predictable."[8] Perhaps, although analysts aren't so glib these days, or at least they shouldn't be. In any case, the habit of labeling economic fluctuations as cyclical is misleading in the 21st century and so we should use the term with caution. The

---

[7] Claessens, et al. (2008), p. 57.

[8] According to Higgins (1985), p.4: "Business cycles before World War II were fairly predictable. The 20 U.S. economic expansions from 1854 to 1933 lasted an average of 25 months, and the corresponding recessions lasted an average of 22 months. Most expansions and recessions during that period were close to the average. Except for wartime buildups, almost 90 percent of expansions lasted one and a half to three years. And about 70 percent of recessions lasted one to two years. The experience gave rise to the belief that the business cycle was regular—perhaps even periodic—with a recession of a little less than two years typically followed by an expansion of about two years."

reference to a cycle implies a steady ebb and flow, such as the regularity of the ocean's tides and the unfolding of the seasons. But the rise and fall of an economy, of course, is erratic, which is why so much time and effort is dedicated to studying and dissecting macro fluctuations.

The only true constant is that growth is followed by recession, which eventually leads to growth, and so on. We can speak of this back and forth as a cycle to facilitate our conversations and writings, but there's precious little in the economy's broad changes that can be called reliably and conspicuously rhythmic. Perhaps the transitory disturbances to growth are a natural adjustment to a real shock; or maybe you're persuaded that recessions are a temporary bout of market failure. But recessions don't arrive on a timetable. By contrast, you can be sure that the debate about the underlying catalysts for these events will rage on with clockwork-like dependability.

If It Walks Like A Duck...

Temporary falls from economic grace are self-evident, but formally defining these events can be tricky. One popular rule of thumb says that a recession is two consecutive quarters of decline in the nation's gross domestic product (GDP), a measure of the value of a nation's output of services and goods. But that definition isn't much help if we're to make any progress in recognizing the risk of downturns on a timely basis. One reason is that quarterly GDP data is published with a substantial lag and so these numbers are of little if any practical use in real time.

How, then, should we characterize an economic recession? NBER recently explained the events as "a significant decline in economic activity spread across the economy, lasting more than a few months, normally visible in production, employment, real income, and other indicators."[9] That sounds reasonable, although it's vague enough to keep a room of economists squabbling for months. No wonder that formal declarations of economic peaks and valleys are publicly dispensed well after the fact. NBER's announcement that the Great Recession started in January 2008, for instance, was noted in a press statement the following December.

Why so long? Part of the answer is that there's plenty of debate in real time about turning points in the business cycle. Reaching consensus takes time. Another factor is NBER's process for recognizing start and end dates for recession—it's a mix of quantitative and qualitative factors, and so there's ample opportunity for gray areas as economists decipher data as it's published. Indeed, most economic reports are revised at least once, sometimes several times. Although there's a short list of indicators that are typically used for dating the business cycle—payrolls and industrial production, for instance—"there is no fixed rule about which other measures may contribute information to the process in any particular episode," NBER explained in a December 2008 statement.[10]

As a timely declaration of when a recession has started, NBER's after-the-fact announcements aren't going to help much. As a record of history and academic analysis, however, NBER-dated recessions are the gold standard for researchers. Indeed, NBER estimates of peaks and troughs are never revised; the goal of

---

[9] "Determination of the December 2007 Peak in Economic Activity" (Dec. 11, 2008), nber.org/cycles/dec2008.html

[10] Ibid.

maintaining that standard helps explain why the group takes its time with choosing start and end dates. If you wait long enough, everything becomes clear. Accordingly, the institution's choices of recession dates line up closely with substantial declines in GDP growth rates through history (Figure 2.2). Equally unsurprising is the fact that NBER's cycle dates are universally recognized as the last word on the phases of expansion and decline for the U.S. In turn, anticipating NBER's future announcements about the start of new recessions provides a roadmap for thinking about how to model, analyze and forecast economic downturns.

Figure 2.2
Real (inflation-adjusted) gross domestic product: % change
from preceding period. Quarterly, seasonally adjusted annual rates.

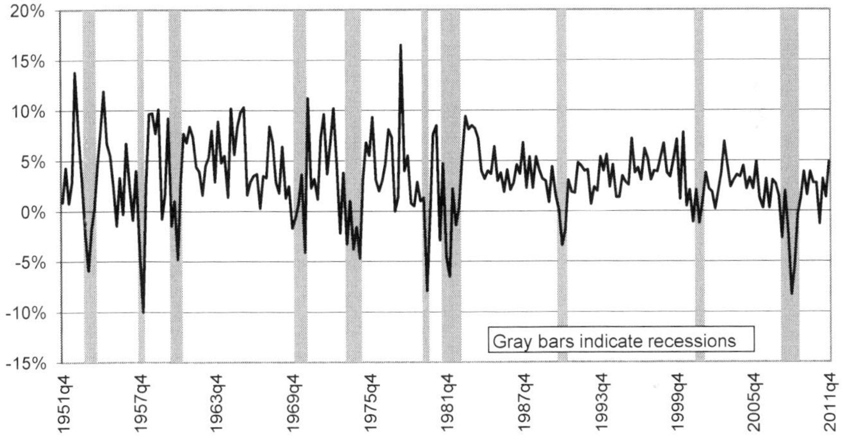

Sources: St. Louis Federal Reserve, NBER

Economists recognize that GDP doesn't have a monopoly on tracking the business cycle. There are numerous proxies of the broad cyclical swings in economic activity that coincide with NBER recession dates. Industrial production and employment growth, for instance, tend to align with NBER peaks and troughs. Consider the most-commonly recognized data series that's associated with recessions by the public: the unemployment rate. Its close association with contractions needs no explanation. The loss of jobs is ground zero for tracking the general sensitivity to economic troubles. The leading empirical fact in business cycle analysis starts with a simple observation: the jobless population rises sharply during NBER-defined recessions (Figure 2.3).

In other words, there's convincing historical evidence for accepting NBER's decisions on cyclical dates. The problem is calling the start date in real time. Waiting for NBER's announcement that a new recession has arrived is about as practical as reading a weather forecast a month after it's been published. That leaves us with the delicate task of deciding if there's a way to replicate NBER's decisions in real time. Can we identify those periods that are *likely* to be named as recessions by NBER in advance of the group's formal declarations? And can we do so with a methodology that's transparent, easily generated via publicly available data in a relatively uncomplicated and reliable format?

The rest of this book will explore the opportunities tied to that question, along with the challenges and risks. The goal is less about forecasting recessions than recognizing—as early as possible, in accordance with the standards above—that a new downturn has become a high-probability event. The good news is that's there's no shortage of research to consider for laying out a plan for making such calls. Indeed, economists in recent years have designed a number of methodologies that attempt to anticipate NBER's decisions. These models draw on the evidence that numerous economic series are useful, in varying degrees, for recognizing heightened recession risk. But it's also clear from studying history that no single indicator is flawless, which inspires the combining of several data sets to minimize the incidence of false signals.

Figure 2.3
Civilian unemployment rate: %, seasonally adjusted, monthly

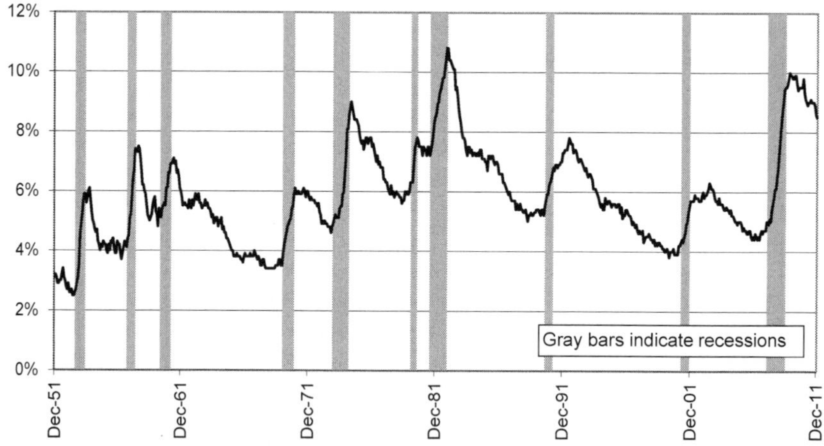

Gray bars indicate recessions

Sources: St. Louis Federal Reserve, NBER

As a simple example, Edward Leamer, an economics professor at UCLA and a research associate at NBER, outlined a straightforward process for anticipating downturns based on three data series that "mimic" NBER's recession-dating announcements. "Most monthly time series are too noisy to serve this function," he explained, "but three do the job rather well: the level of payroll employment, the level of industrial production and the rate of unemployment." New recessions, based on NBER dates, "conform closely to periods of falling payroll employment, falling industrial production and rising unemployment."[11]

Figure 2.4 compares the three series listed by Leamer and tracks their histories from the mid-1980s, based on rolling one-year percentage changes for industrial

---

[11] Leamer (2008), p. 8.

production and payrolls, along with the inverted values for the jobless rate. The chart provides visual confirmation that the trio has an encouraging history of capturing what we think of as the business cycle.

Figure 2.4
Annual % changes in industrial production, nonfarm payrolls,
and unemployment rate (inverted), monthly

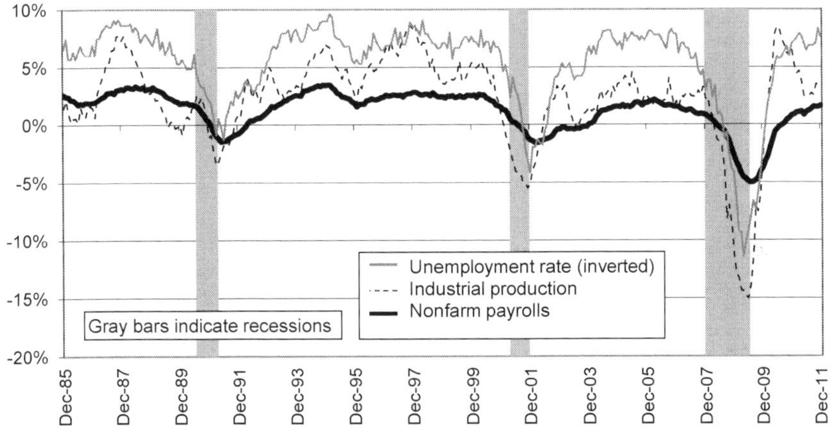

Sources: St. Louis Federal Reserve, NBER

For another view of the connection between the economic indicators analyzed by Leamer, consider how annual changes for industrial production compare with one-year fluctuations in nonfarm payrolls by way of an ordinary least squares regression. Figure 2.5 illustrates rather persuasively that falling industrial output coincides closely with declining employment, and vice versa. The overall trend, summarized by the upward-sloping black line in Figure 2.5, translates into a relatively high R-squared reading of roughly 0.66 for the two data sets.[12] Statistically speaking, this relationship implies that rises and falls in one economic measure are likely to be accompanied by comparable moves in the other.

But it's also clear that different indicators impart varying degrees of insight, at different times, for measuring and interpreting the broad economic trend through time. For example, a 2008 study by the International Monetary Fund found that credit crunches, equity market busts, and house price declines are "associated" with 76 out of 122 recessions in countries around the world across nearly a half century through 2007. "In about one out of six recessions, there is also a credit crunch underway and in about one out of four recessions, also a house price bust," the IMF reported. "Equity price busts overlap for about one-third of recession episodes."[13]

---

[12] R-squared is a statistical measure that quantifies how closely the data are fitted to the regression line. Readings for R-squared range from 0 to 1.0. Higher values indicate a stronger relationship. A 1.0 level signals a perfect fit; a reading of zero indicates no relationship in the data.

[13] Claessens, et al. (2008), pp. 13-14.

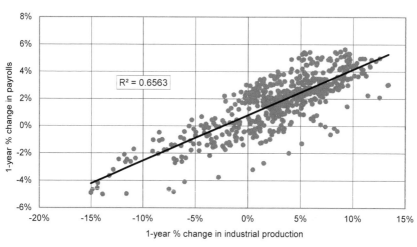

Figure 2.5
1-year % changes: industrial production vs. nonfarm payrolls: 1961-2011

$R^2 = 0.6563$

1-year % change in payrolls

1-year % change in industrial production

Source: St. Louis Federal Reserve

But history isn't a perfect guide to the future. The intuition for using several economic series arises from the likelihood, if not the inevitability, that one or more predictors will mislead us at times in the task of evaluating recession risk. No one knows which indicator (or indicators) will fail in providing an early clue of trouble the next time macro trouble arises. It's only prudent to assume that perfection will forever be elusive, no matter how carefully we select a portfolio of indicators. History certainly advises us to assume no less. Developing expectations based on a diversified set of numbers is therefore essential.

The modern rationale for combining individual signals in search of a higher level of reliability can be traced to seminal papers in the late-1960s that laid the foundation for using a variety of predictions to manage forecasting risk.[14] Subsequent studies over the years have used this research for extending the basic concept into various areas of econometric analysis. "The results have been virtually unanimous: combining multiple forecasts leads to increased forecast accuracy," Robert Clemen opined in a 1989 review of the literature. "In many cases one can make dramatic performance improvements by simply averaging the forecasts."[15]

The literature that Clemen reviewed focused on forecasts rather than the data per se. But it's a natural leap from combining predictions to merging economic time series to improve the value of the signal. For example, economists James Stock and Mark Watson recognized that asset prices are a useful resource for evaluating the economic outlook, although "instability of predictive relations based on asset prices (like many other candidate leading indicators) is the norm," they reminded in a 2003 paper. At the same time, "simple methods for combining the information in the

---

[14] See Reid (1968) and Bates and Granger (1969) for early examples of combining forecasts.
[15] Clemen (1989), p. 559.

various predictors, such as computing the median of a panel of forecasts based on individual asset prices, seem to circumvent the worst of these instability problems."[16]

Indeed, a number of studies show that the Treasury yield curve (the difference between long and short interest rates on government securities) has a constructive track record for anticipating recessions. Yet the value of the yield curve as a forward-looking metric is flawed at times. Fortunately, its signals about the future can be strengthened by considering additional variables, such as the stock market and broadly defined measures of economic growth.[17] A 2007 study by researchers at the Federal Reserve noted that monitoring the spreads of corporate interest rates *and* the Treasury yield curve reduces the "false positive" forecasts compared with looking at the government yield curve alone.[18]

Leading The Way
There are two basic methods for improving forecasts, according to Munechika Katayama, an economics professor at Louisiana State University. One is searching for a superior set of indicators; the other is deciding how to combine indicators to generate optimal forecasts. In a 2010 study, he tested both strategies and reviewed the prediction histories of several models that rely on various combinations of more than 30 economic variables. He discovered that "the combination of the term spread between 10-year Treasury yield and the Federal Funds rate, changes in the S&P 500, and non-farm employment growth outperforms other variable combinations in the out-of-sample forecasting exercise."[19]

Keeping an eye out for early signs of business cycle turning points by analyzing multiple economic series and testing various combinations is hardly a new idea in macro. Wesley Mitchell and Arthur Burns forged the path decades ago and in the late-1930s came up with the idea of what's known as leading indicators. The concept has been more or less under revision ever since.[20] In the 21st century, economists have developed a number of benchmarks that take a page from Mitchell and Burns' pioneering work.[21] The common theme is that a select group of indicators can dispense warning signs before the macro deterioration is obvious in the economy overall. Economic indicators, in other words, aren't created equal as tools for analyzing recession risk.

Looking for clues about the outlook for the broad trend starts by distinguishing leading from coincident and lagging indicators, advised Wesley Mitchell and Arthur Burns in a famous research note from 1938,[22] which forged an idea that was fully developed in their subsequent and highly influential 1946 book *Measuring Business Cycles*.[23] A large portion of the dismal science continues to embrace the concept that

---

[16] Stock and Watson (2003), p. 789.
[17] Estrella and Mishkin (1998).
[18] King, et al. (2007).
[19] Katayama (2010), p. 37.
[20] See Achuthan and Banerji (2004), Crone (2006), and Stock and Watson (1989) for related analysis and commentary.
[21] Examples include Aruoba, et al. (2009), Chauvet and Hamilton (2006), Dueker (2005), and Wildi (2009).
[22] Mitchell and Burns (1938).
[23] Burns and Mitchell (1946).

leading indicators will provide early tips when trouble is brewing. The reasoning is that a true leading indicator will, in theory, offer forward guidance because it anticipates the future behavior of coincident indicators, which are considered measures of an economy's current state.

As an example, consider how one pair of leading and coincident indexes fared going into the Great Recession of 2008-2009 (Figure 2.6), based on revised data.[24] Note that in this case the leading index started declining well before its coincident counterpart began to slump. An early warning is exactly what we should expect from leading indicators.

Figure 2.6
Philadelphia Fed's Leading and Coincident Economic Activity Indicators

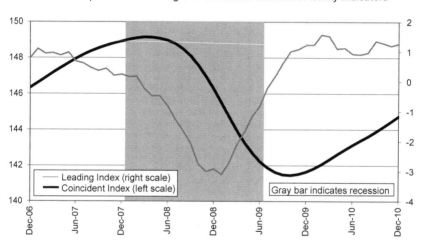

Sources: St. Louis Federal Reserve, Philadelphia Federal Reserve, NBER

The true meaning of the real-time signals is only obvious with the benefit of hindsight, however. The challenge of distinguishing noise from valid warnings can't be underestimated as a real-time exercise. When a leading indicator is falling, it's never immediately clear if it's reflecting short-term volatility in an otherwise ongoing expansion vs. the start of a new recession. Full clarity arrives eventually, by way of the coincident indicator's behavior, but that takes time. In the interim, analysts are always struggling to interpret the signals as the numbers are reported.

For instance, the decline in the Philadelphia Fed's leading index in 2007 and early 2008 in Figure 2.6 was all but confirmed as the start of a new recession once the coincident index had been sliding consistently by the second half of 2008. A relatively high degree of clarity can't be rushed. The evidence of a new recession

---

[24] A leading *index* here and throughout refers to a benchmark that reflects the aggregation of several individual leading indicators. For instance, averaging the year-over-year percentage changes for initial jobless claims and the stock market can be defined as a leading index.

accumulates gradually, over months. But waiting for confirmation from leading indicators can eat up precious time. There's also the question of how to build an index of leading indicators (or how to choose from among the various benchmarks that make the choices for you). One set of leading and coincident indicators may outperform another, but it's hard to know if that's just luck or superior design. What we do know is that the track record with these benchmarks is far from consistently reliable. It doesn't help that a considerable amount of subjective analysis may be required for deciphering leading- and coincident-indicator benchmarks in real time.

Between an initial downturn of a leading indicator and the subsequent confirmation (or rejection) with a coincident indicator, there's always debate about the true signal. The rush to judgment is an ever-present danger when we don't know the outcome. In time, the evidence is convincingly persuasive, one way or another. In the weeks and months leading up to that point, the focus is usually one of looking for a tipping point that marks the start of a new downturn.

A leading indicator can, in theory, offer guidance because it's supposed to predict the behavior of coincident indicators. But the obvious question arises: How reliable are leading indicators? Like everything else in economics, the answer depends on the details, starting with the index's design and how one interprets the movements. Even under the best of circumstances, there will be limits on what can be achieved. Victor Zarnowitz, another pioneer in the empirical school of business cycle analysis during the 20th century, pointed out three primary challenges that bedevil the forecaster's job of calling major turning points for an economy:

- The predictive value of any one indicator fluctuates through time.
- Economic data is subject to revision and so initial signals can be misleading.
- Short-term statistical noise, due to temporary effects such as weather, labor strikes, etc., can cloud forecast accuracy.[25]

Playing Defense

Fortunately, there are defensive responses to these analytical challenges, starting with the use of a diversified mix of indicators. For the problem of errors in the preliminary economic reports, we can design leading indexes that use several indicators that are independent of one another so that any errors are likely to be independent as well. In that case, errors are more likely to cancel out one another, or at least inflict minimal damage on the overall signal. We can also use indicators that aren't subject to revision, such as stock market returns and interest-rate spreads for bonds. As Zarnowitz explained, "By combining the series into an index, some of that noise is eliminated; that is, a well-constructed composite index can be much smoother than any of its components."[26]

Another defensive technique is comparing several leading and coincident indexes. This can be especially useful when reviewing benchmarks of substantially different designs. In that case, three leadings indexes that are warning of elevated recession risk is a stronger signal than a prediction of danger from one index.

---

[25] Summarized from Zarnowitz (1992), pp. 316-319.
[26] Ibid., p. 317.

We can also keep an eye on what's known as potential GDP as a rough measure for evaluating the relevance of a given recession warning. The logic here is that the economy has a theoretical maximum output level. Actual output can surpass this theoretical limit for a brief time—a positive output gap. Eventually, however, the natural ceiling for an economy running at or near full speed acts as a brake on growth. In those periods when actual GDP exceeds potential GDP, the risk of a cyclical slowdown is relatively high if trouble arrives, such as a spike in oil prices or another event that creates a new headwind.[27]

The economy's potential output is in constant flux, of course, although the general trend (in line with actual GDP) is positive, which reflects a rising population, growth in the supply of investment capital, technological innovation, etc. This theoretical limit "is not a technical ceiling on output that cannot be exceeded," noted a paper from the Congressional Budget Office. "Rather, it is a measure of maximum sustainable output—the level of real GDP in a given year that is consistent with a stable rate of inflation. If actual output rises above its potential level, then constraints on capacity begin to bind and inflationary pressures build; if output falls below potential, then resources are lying idle and inflationary pressures abate."[28]

Consider how the ratio of actual to potential GDP compares with recessions through the decades (Figure 2.7).[29] Note that actual GDP relative to potential GDP tends to be relatively high just ahead of economic slumps. In nine of the last 10 recessions, actual economic output exceeded potential output (indicated by a reading above 1.0). The 1981-1982 recession is the lone exception. In that case, the recession began with a ratio under 1.0 (a negative output gap), although that outlier event may be the result of a) the economy hadn't fully recovered from the previous recession; and b) the interim period of growth between the two recessions was relatively short. In any case, it's reasonable to assume that recession warnings are stronger in periods of positive output gaps—i.e., the ratio of real actual GDP to real potential GDP is above 1.0.[30]

---

[27] The idea that an economy has a theoretical level of potential output is credited as the brainchild of economist Arthur Okun, who introduced the idea in a 1962 paper. "Potential GNP is a supply concept, a measure of productive capacity," he wrote. The operative question that the concept seeks to answer, he explained: "How much output can the economy produce under conditions of full employment?" ("Potential GNP: Its Measurement and Significance," reprinted as Cowles Foundation Paper 190: cowles.econ.yale.edu/P/cp/p01b/p0190.pdf)

[28] Congressional Budget Office (2001), p. 1. For additional perspective on potential GDP and the business cycle, including a short bibliography on the subject, see Weidner and Williams (2009): "The output gap measures how far the economy is from its full employment or 'potential' level that depends on supply-side factors of the economy: the supply of workers and their productivity. During a boom, economic activity may for a time rise above this potential level and the output gap is positive. During a recession, the economy drops below its potential level and the output gap is negative.... A positive output gap implies an overheating economy and upward pressure on inflation. A negative output gap implies a slack economy and downward pressure on inflation."

[29] Figure 2.7 reflects data that was compiled before the U.S. Bureau of Economic Analysis published a comprehensive revision of its GDP data series on July 31, 2013.

[30] There are several formulas for calculating potential GDP. In Figure 2.7, I use potential GDP estimates based on the methodology in Congressional Budget Office (2001). The underlying data for computing the ratio is available at St. Louis Federal Reserve's FRED database

Figure 2.7
Ratio of Real GDP to Potential GDP

Sources: St. Louis Federal Reserve, Congressional Budget Office

But let's not kid ourselves about the difficulty of finding clear signals. No matter how clever the analysis, no matter how enlightened a model's design, some hazards can't be controlled. First and foremost, the optimal set of indicators for the period ahead is always ambiguous. Studying history can guide us, but the value of each data series is always changing. No wonder that leading indexes are subject to revision and subjective interpretation. That inspires rethinking and revising methodologies that were previously deemed sufficient. In January 2012, for example, the Conference Board modified its widely followed leading economic index—the "first comprehensive revision" since 1996. The adjustment "addresses the structural changes that have occurred in the U.S. economy in the last several decades," the Conference Board explained.[31]

We should never lose sight of the fact that there are hard limits to breaking the lock on uncertainty and surprise. The further out in time we look, the more we rely on subjective interpretation, assumption, and outright speculation. All of which implies that there's substantial risk in forecasting much beyond a few months.

A recent study of the forecasting skills of several leading indicators found that ten months ahead is the outer range for anticipating major turning points in the business cycle with any confidence.[32] But even gazing that far out may be expecting too much in terms of what can reliably be discerned. A lot can (and often does) arise across a 10-month window of time, and quite a lot of it will be surprising in some degree. It's safer to argue that our capacity for looking ahead is limited to two or three months at most.

(research.stlouisfed.org): Real Gross Domestic Product, 1 Decimal (GDPC1) and Real Potential Gross Domestic Product (GDPPOT). Also, see footnote 28 above.

[31] Levanon, et al. (2011), p. 1.

[32] See Berge and Jorda (2010) and Berge and Jorda (2012) for details.

Some analysts are reluctant to even go that far and instead recommend that spotting a new recession in its early stages—after it's started but before it's widely recognized—is the best we can hope for. That's the premise of this book. Forecasting is fine—used prudently, it can be a productive tool to *supplement* our analysis. But forecasting, by its nature, is subject to a high degree of error and should be used sparingly, if at all. We simply don't know what future events will be or how they might transform what appears to be a reasonable forecast into garbage. That doesn't stop the world from spitting out predictions in copious quantities. What's in short supply is objective context for assessing recession risk based on the numbers in hand (as opposed to the guesses du jour about the future).

As it turns out, a prudent review of a broad spectrum of economic and financial market data has an encouraging history of alerting us fairly early with signs that the economy has recently peaked. Reviewing and analyzing the process for developing this strategic information is the focus for the remainder of this book.

You Really Can See A Lot By Looking

But you can't see much of anything if you're not paying attention to the details. In particular, it's hard to develop a high degree of confidence about what the numbers are telling us without spending time with the data and reviewing economic and financial history. That inspires a closer look at the short list of leading and coincident indicators in an effort to develop a deeper understanding of how these metrics ebb and flow with the onset of recessions. Historical context can help us interpret the business cycle in real time… up to a point. But there's always—*always*—room for debate and doubt.

"There is no single proven and accepted cause of all observed business cycles," Zarnowitz counseled. "Instead, there are a number of plausible and not mutually exclusive hypotheses about what can cause downturns and contractions, upturns and expansions." It follows, then, that "no single chain of symptoms exists that would invariably presage these developments. Instead, there are a number of frequently observed regularities that seem likely to persist and play important roles in business cycles but are certainly not immutable."[33]

That means that we must routinely, systematically, and intelligently evaluate risk using a diversified mix of data. We never know when any one indicator is dispensing deceptive signals. The only solution: build an expansive proxy of the cycle in order to minimize the chance of failure that can arise from one or even several metrics.

And so it's time to examine the building blocks for measuring recession risk by studying each of the key indicators in some detail. Afterward, we'll combine the indicators in search of an aggregate measure for analyzing economic volatility. As you'll see, a straightforward system that's designed to capture a broad measure of the economy can tell us quite a lot—more, in fact, than is generally recognized. But in order to fully appreciate such a gauge, and develop confidence in its signals, it's essential to review how it's built and the rationale behind the design.

Let's begin with everyone's favorite discounting machine… the stock market.

---

[33] Zarnowitz (1992), p. 316.

PART II

ECONOMIC INDICATORS

Chapter 3

The Predictions of Crowds & "Soulless Barometers"

The stock market

The business cycle casts a long shadow over market prices, but the relationship is a two-way street. Financial markets also drop clues about the state of the economy. Together, this pair offers more opportunity for mining strategic intelligence compared with looking at either one in isolation.

Does that sound familiar? It should. The idea that the economy and the markets are complimentary for analytical purposes has some mileage. The economist Irving Fisher, for example, profiled a connection between short-term interest rates and economic expectations in his 1907 book *The Rate of Interest.*[1]

There's no record of what William Peter Hamilton thought of Fisher's idea, but he probably would have embraced a theory that found value in looking to financial data for anticipating macro conditions. As editor of *The Wall Street Journal* in the first three decades of the 20th century, Hamilton outlined the case for looking to the stock market as a barometer for measuring the business cycle. Hamilton is best remembered for enhancing the finer points of the so-called Dow Theory, the market-timing system that was invented by Charles Dow, the *Journal*'s founder who also created the first stock market index, the Dow Jones Industrial Average. Reviewing the nexus between the economy and the market, Hamilton advised in 1922:

> What we need are soulless barometers, price indexes and averages to tell us where we are going and what we may expect. The best, because the most impartial, the most remorseless of these barometers, is the recorded average of prices in the stock exchange.[2]

In the years that followed, researchers continued to investigate the dance between markets and macro. On the eve of World War Two, economists Wesley Mitchell and Arthur Burns introduced the leading indicator concept—a set of economic signals that are expected to drop clues about the future path of the economy. Summarizing the project, they wrote that "what we have to offer is a digest of past experience, which we take to be on the whole the best teacher of what to expect in the near future."[3] Anyone who's familiar with Hamilton's writings shouldn't be surprised to learn that Burns and Mitchell chose the Dow Jones Industrials as one of several leading indicators in their 1938 study. The tradition continued in the 21st century and

---

[1] Harvey (1988) explained that "the link between asset markets and real economic growth was formalized by Irving Fisher," who suggested that "in equilibrium, the one-year interest rate reflects the marginal value of income today in relation to its marginal value next year." Fisher's theory "implies that current real interest rates contain information about expected economic growth," Harvey advised (p. 38).

[2] Hamilton (1922), p. 4.

[3] Mitchell and Burns (1938), p. 1.

the S&P 500 stock index remains one of several gauges in the Conference Board's Leading Economic Index.

Equity prices provide valuable clues for estimating the economic outlook, but the signals that arise from Mr. Market's gyrations can never be blindly accepted as gospel. One of the 20th century's giants in the dismal science said as much in a widely repeated quote. Paul Samuelson, the first American to win the Nobel prize for economics, quipped that "the stock market has predicted nine of the last five recessions."[4]

The equity market is no one's idea of an infallible crystal ball, but Samuelson's endlessly quoted grievance, while grounded in truth, popularized the idea that because the market can be wrong it can never be right. His comment also planted the seed that nothing less than perfection must be our guide for choosing indicators to help us make assumptions about the economy. That's an impossible standard, of course, and it leaves us with no choice other than to passively accept our fate as economic history rolls on (and over us).

Fortunately, there's another path, and one that can be productive: combine the stock market's signals with other indicators to create a more reliable gauge of recession risk. Any lone variable is subject to erroneous messages at times, and the stock market is no exception. But the mistake that some critics make is rejecting an indicator because it's flawed. Well, they're all flawed. But if we're searching for relatively reliable signals about the business cycle, we can learn quite a lot by combining flawed indicators. If we're diligent in choosing and mixing—using the economic literature as a guide—we can develop quite a lot of valuable context in our quest to evaluate the state of macro risk. An obvious place to start: the stock market.

A Natural Relationship

Looking to equities for assessing the economic cycle is a natural extension of asset pricing theory. The idea also draws on common sense too. As an economist once explained, "stock prices rise because of higher expected corporate earnings or because of a lower required rate of return used by investors to discount earnings."[5] Okay, but why do earnings bounce around? All explanations ultimately lead us back to the business cycle.

The transmission channel from the economy to equity prices can take many forms, of course. And just to keep things interesting, there are several complicating factors to ensure that the relationship is dynamic and not necessarily transparent in the short term. Changes in investor psychology, for instance, influence expectations as expressed through fluctuations in asset prices. Keynes recognized as much with his "animal spirits" metaphor for explaining how emotions drive financial and economic decisions.

A more-recent view incorporates the so-called wealth effect into the analysis. One theory emphasized how changing stock prices impact spending habits. Investors feel more or less wealthy, depending on market conditions. The resulting shift in sentiment, if it's strong enough, can alter the course of the economy. At least one

---

[4] *Newsweek*, September 19, 1966
[5] Pearce (1983), p. 8.

study found a "direct" link between consumption patterns for U.S. households that held equity investments and the stock market.[6]

Numerous researchers over the years have uncovered similar connections. One outline that's become widely accepted is that the equity risk premium varies countercyclically with the economy.[7] Expected returns are higher during recessions, and lower in economic expansions—a relationship that has traction in several studies.[8] The crowd is forever looking ahead, according to this line of analysis. That's no assurance that the market is always right about what comes next. In fact, you can count on the market being wrong a fair amount of the time. But over the grand sweep of history, Mr. Market's forecasts are a valuable tool for gazing forward.

Professor Eugene Fama of efficient-market-theory fame, for instance, discovered that stock returns are linked with future levels of industrial production.[9] A follow-up study confirmed Fama's results by using a different data set over a longer period of time, starting in 1889. "There is a strong positive relation between real stock returns and future production growth," William Schwert reported. "Although there are many reasons that stock returns could be related to future real [economic] activity, the fact that these relations show up in 100 years of data strengthens Fama's conclusions" while virtually ruling out data mining as the cause.[10]

Economist Jeremy Siegel, a leading authority on the stock market's historical record, cut to the chase and advised that the equity market has "held the role of the most sensitive indicator of the business cycle."[11]

Ongoing research has continued to support this narrative. One recent review found a strong set of links between changes in asset prices, investment (real private nonresidential fixed investment), and the broad economy (real gross domestic product). "These patterns of the business cycle can be consistent with the standard view that asset prices reflect expectations about the future health of the aggregate economy," according to a 2011 study.[12] A few years earlier, the research team of Stock and Watson advised that the price-discovery process is closely bound up with forward-looking markets. "The premise that interest rates and asset prices contain useful information about future economic developments embodies foundational concepts of macroeconomics," they explained.[13] Another study demonstrated that equity returns, changes in the Treasury yield curve, and excess returns in several

---

[6] See Dynan and Maki (2001), who wrote (p. 25): "Our results imply the aggregate relationship between consumption and stock market wealth is consistent with a 'direct' view of wealth effects, in which changes in total consumption stem from changes in the consumption of households that own stocks. The consumption growth of Consumer Expenditure Survey households holding securities has a strong positive correlation with both contemporaneous and lagged movements in stock prices."

[7] See Ferson and Harvey (1991), for example.

[8] Examples include Chen (1991), Moller and Sander (2013), Pastor and Stambaugh (2001).

[9] Fama (1990).

[10] Schwert (1990), p. 1256.

[11] Siegel (1991), p. 27.

[12] Shi (2011), p. 1.

[13] Stock and Watson (2003), p. 788.

asset classes are positively correlated with future economic growth. The stock market, for instance, has a habit of anticipating declines in industrial production.[14]

But the coupling of academic models with the empirical record can be problematic for any one moment in time. What's true for the broad sweep of history doesn't always play out neatly in any given month or year. The real world is messy and so theories are only a guide. Asset prices contain information for predicting the business cycle, but the forecasting ability of any one variable can be unstable under certain conditions, particularly in the short run.

Keeping the limitations of gazing forward in mind, market data should be considered an aid for making decisions about what's likely to unfold rather than as the sole arbiter for thinking about the economy. One reason to look to equity prices cautiously as an analytical tool for judging macro is the short-term volatility that regularly rocks the market—volatility that's not always related to major turning points in the business cycle. The good news is that we can filter out some of this short-term noise by looking at annual changes in the market. In fact, reviewing year-over-year changes promotes clarity for most of the data sets that we'll use for evaluating recession risk in the chapters ahead. But for the moment, let's stick with the equity market.

Figure 3.1
12-month % price change for U.S. stocks (S&P 500) vs.
year-ahead 12-month % change for U.S. private nonfarm payrolls

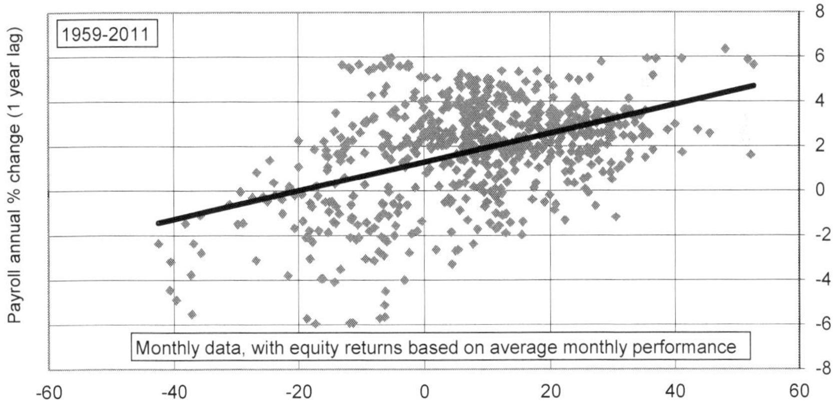

Stock market annual % change

Source: St. Louis Fed, author

Filtering Volatility Through An Annual Lens

Consider 12-month percentage changes in the stock market (S&P 500) with year-ahead 12-month percentage changes in private-sector payrolls, a proxy for the business cycle (Figure 3.1). In other words, the stock market data lags by one year relative to the employment numbers, i.e., the current payrolls change is matched with

---

[14] Backus, et. al (2010), p. 1.

the year-earlier change in equities. The intuition here is that if equity prices are lower today (relative to year-ago levels), that implies that the economy will weaken in the near-term future. The fact that annual losses in the stock market are relatively rare strengthens the case for thinking that red ink on an annual basis imparts valuable information. In that case, we should expect employment levels to fall soon after those times when the stock market performance turns negative on an annual basis.

Reviewing this history across decades does in fact show a relationship, but one that's also prone to a fair amount of noise. The stock market appears partly sensitive to future changes in payroll employment, as Figure 3.1 suggests. Alas, you won't find pinpoint accuracy here. The linear regression for these two variables shows an R-squared of roughly 0.21 for the half century through the end of 2011. In other words, red ink for stocks on a year-over-year basis has only a loose connection with anticipating a weak labor market in the near-term future.

Figure 3.2
Cross Correlations: US Stock Market & Private Nonfarm Payrolls
based on annual % changes (1958 - 2011)

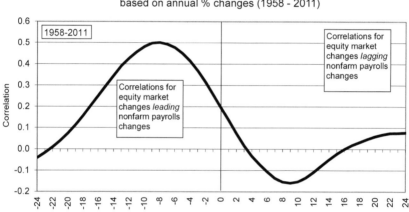

Sources: St. Louis Fed and CapitalSpectator.com

The connection between stocks and subsequent economic activity may be wobbly, but let's not be too hasty. Full clarity about the future is always elusive, no matter the data set or analytical technique. But let's consider another perspective. Figure 3.2 shows a fluctuating relationship between annual changes in equities and payrolls. This relationship is strongest in terms of the current state of the stock market relative to the labor market's changes eight to nine months in the future, as indicated by the peak correlation reading of 0.5 on the left-hand side of Figure 3.2.[15] By contrast, there appears to be no relationship between the stock market's current annual change in connection with payroll changes 24 months in the future, as

---

[15] Correlation is a statistical measure of the relationship between two data sets. Correlation values range from -1 to +1 (perfect negative or positive correlation, respectively). Values between those extremes reflect grades of positive and negative correlation.

suggested by the relatively low correlation reading of 0.08 on the far right in Figure 3.2.[16]

The lesson is that the relationship between the stock market and future activity in payrolls (and other economic indicators) is stronger at certain points than others. Unfortunately, it's never strong enough to use in isolation as a high-confidence signal for recession risk at all times. Maybe that's because the economy is in a growth mode most of the time. In any case, the stock market is continually buffeted by speculative forces in the short run—forces that don't routinely correspond with major changes in macroeconomic conditions.

We should be skeptical of the stock market's powers for evaluating the economy as a general rule. But let's also recognize that at the extremes the relationship provides stronger signals. In particular, the relatively rare instances of deep annual losses in the stock market often reflect the elevated odds of recession risk.

Mr. Market's Recession Forecasts
A casual review of the U.S. stock market and the start date of recessions since the late-1800s shows that equity prices usually reach a cyclical peak in advance of contractions.[17] It's not a perfect record, but it's sufficiently persistent to inspire watching the broad trend in equities for early signs of economic distress. The problem is that market tops are obvious only in hindsight. Confidently labeling a peak in equity prices as the genuine article, rather than short-term noise, can take many months to rule out that there's more than short-term volatility in play.

Obviously, we need a more reliable way to measure the market's relationship with the business cycle than simply looking for peaks in equity prices. As suggested above, one useful metric is the 12-month percentage change (Figure 3.3). Given the stock market's long-term upward bias, one-year returns are usually positive. In those rare instances when performance turns negative on a year-over-year basis (based on average monthly prices), it's usually a reflection of trouble brewing in the broader economy.[18] The stock market can turn negative on an annual basis for any number of reasons, but history also reminds us that whenever we see red ink on a year-over-year basis there's good reason to suspect that the loss may be a sign that the business cycle is in trouble.

---

[16] For a detailed analysis of the cross correlations data that's focused on the financial markets and the economy, see Backus, et al. (2010).

[17] This record is based on analyzing recessions since 1873 in context with the stock market history as compiled by Professor Robert Shiller of Yale. His database (www.econ.yale.edu/~shiller/) reports average monthly prices starting in January 1871 for the S&P 500 and its predecessor indices.

[18] Here and throughout I use average monthly prices for the stocks (S&P 500) for calculating annual percentage returns. Annual changes based on daily prices is an alternative methodology, but this approach can suffer from a high level of short-term noise, which is problematic for assessing the less-frequently updated economic indicators. Another possibility is using monthly data based on month-end prices, but this choice puts too much emphasis on individual trading sessions, which can also distort the analysis because of short-term volatility at the end of a month that may be unrelated to economic conditions. Focusing on average monthly prices, as computed by the St. Louis Fed's FRED database, is a reasonable compromise for evaluating the stocks for signs of recession risk.

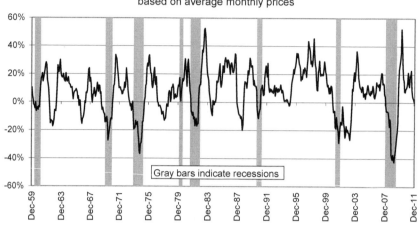

Figure 3.3
Rolling 12-month % price change for U.S. stocks (S&P 500),
based on average monthly prices

Sources: St. Louis Federal Reserve, NBER, James Picerno

Note the tendency for stocks to post annual losses in the early stages of recession, or just ahead of economic downturns. For example, the equity market's year-over-year price performance slipped to a loss shortly before the start of four downturns over the past half century: 1960, 1970, 1974, and 2001. For another three recessions (1981, 1990 and 2008), the red ink arrived simultaneously with the onset of the slump. The outlier is 1980, when the stock market's annual gain decelerated but never moved to a loss. Perhaps that unusual scenario is related to the brief duration of the 1980 recession.[19] The 1980 exception aside, it's fair to say that equity prices are sensitive to recession risk.

In fact, Mr. Market's track record is quite impressive when you consider that stocks often catch wind of recession risk earlier compared with the gazing eyes of many economists. Consider the onset of the Great Recession, which started in January 2008. A number of analysts (and a fair share of investors) were anxious about the economic outlook in the early days of that fateful year. But the expectation that a recession was near was far from widely accepted at the time. Fed Chairman Ben Bernanke, for one, remained cautiously optimistic shortly after the start of 2008. With the benefit of hundreds of staff economists to draw on, the leader of the world's most important central bank told the press on January 10 that "the Federal Reserve is not currently forecasting a recession."[20] The stock market was suggesting otherwise, based on negative annual returns that took on a deepening shade of red

---

[19] At the end of February 1980, a month that marked the start of a new recession, the S&P 500's 12-month price return was a lofty 17.4%; two months later, at April's close, the annual change was less than 1%. In another three months, July 1980, the recession ended, as NBER eventually announced.

[20] http://www.nbcnews.com/id/22592939/#.UmrokRCx1XQ

throughout most of that month. For the final tally in January, the S&P 500's annual performance was -3.2%, based on average monthly prices—the first year-over-year decline in nearly five years. In the months ahead, the 12-month return on the S&P 500 slipped further below zero, offering a stronger statistical case for anticipating an economic contraction.[21]

It's true that as early as 2007 there were some economists warning that recession risk was rising. But many more were late to the party, offering varying rationales for thinking optimistically—right up to the point when even casual observation could no longer ignore what had become obvious.

Dissent among dismal scientists isn't unusual at major turning points in the cycle, but the cacophony of competing predictions can be confusing. One of the benefits of using Mr. Market's equity forecasts: they're transparent, available in real time, immune to revision, free, and fairly reliable when judged across history. Some pundits are quick to dismiss the market as a forecasting yardstick, but most economists would love to have a track record that compared as favorably as the 12-month price change that equities claim for anticipating a downturn.

The problem is that the equity market has been known to anticipate a recession that never materializes. Annual losses in stocks don't always coincide with NBER-verified economic slumps. But even here the oversights may be less egregious than they appear to be at first review. In some cases, the threat of recession was clearly elevated and so the market's tumble was partly justified, even though a formal recession never arrived. In 1966, for example, a "credit crunch" hit the U.S., unleashing the "first financial crisis of the postwar period," according to Martin Wolfson in his book *Financial Crises*.[22] The rate of economic growth slowed considerably as 1966 progressed. By the year's second quarter, real annualized growth decelerated to a only 1.6%—a fraction of the roaring 10.3% rise in the previous three-month period, according to the U.S. Bureau of Economic Analysis. The slowdown continued, and by the second quarter of 1967 economic growth came to a virtual halt, with real gross domestic product advancing by a thin 0.3%. Nonetheless, the next formal recession didn't start until January 1970, as per NBER. As a result, the stock market's year-over-year decline in the second-half of 1966 was technically wrong as a business cycle indicator.

We may be able to excuse some of the market's false warnings when the risk of recession appears to be on the march, even if the hazard never goes terminal and leads to a broad-scale decline in output. But some instances of market tumbles are

---

[21] This is a good point for a brief digression on measuring the stock market's performance for signs of recession risk. In particular, why choose a 12-month return using average monthly prices? Why not six or 18 months? And why not use month-end prices rather than average monthly prices? The short answer is that we're looking for signals that balance the conflicting problems of timeliness vs. noise. Focusing on signals that are overly dependent on recent history leaves us vulnerable to the random fluctuations that hamper the search for the broader trend. At the other extreme, emphasizing time frames that are too long leaves us vulnerable to the risk of overlooking the critical signals on a timely basis. A one-year time horizon is a reasonable compromise, although a deeper study of searching for the optimal period may yield superior results—a task I leave to others. Meantime, the use of average monthly data, as opposed to month-end prices, is a practical attempt at smoothing out the short-term noise that can arise when relying on daily data points.

[22] Wolfson (1986), p. 41.

harder if not impossible to rationalize. The 1987 stock market crash, in particular, is especially difficult to defend. The extraordinary one-day loss of 20%-plus on October 19 reverberated for months, leaving the S&P 500 with steep annual losses well into 1988. Some economists claim that the crash reflected legitimate concerns about the economic outlook, although a widely accepted explanation for the selling blames institutional trading programs that ran amuck. In any case, the wave of one-day selling didn't lead to a recession and so the market's fears, reasonable or not, were misplaced in terms of what actually came to pass.

That's a reminder that Samuelson's famous warning can't be dismissed. A 12-month loss for stocks doesn't guarantee that a new downturn is near. But it's also true that every recession in the last 50 years has been accompanied by a 12-month decline in stock prices overall. The message is that recessions and annual losses in stocks go hand in hand. Exactly when the market picks up on recession risk will vary, perhaps widely, but it's still foolish to overlook this "soulless barometer."

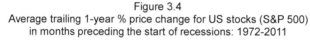

Figure 3.4
Average trailing 1-year % price change for US stocks (S&P 500)
in months preceding the start of recessions: 1972-2011

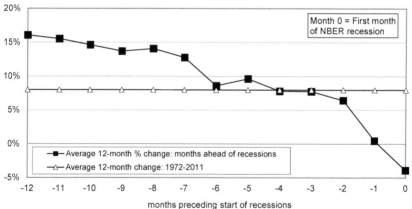

Sources: St. Louis Federal Reserve, NBER, James Picerno

Consider how annual changes in the market compare, on average, through the decades during the 12 months leading up to the onset on recessions (Figure 3.4). In the months just ahead of economic contractions, annual gains in equities tend to fade. Indeed, the average change in the month before the official start of recessions (indicated by -1 on the horizontal axis in Figure 3.4) is virtually flat. Once the recession formally begins (month 0), the annual change for stocks slips to a 3.9% loss on average. To put this in perspective, the annual gain for equities across time is 7.9%, based on the rolling average of 12-month returns for 1972-2011 (the period covered in Figure 3.4).

The key point is that every recession is associated with annual market losses in recent history, but not every annual equity market loss is linked with recession.

That's a strong reminder that we can't afford to ignore the market's year-over-year fluctuations when it comes to assessing recession risk. At the same time, we can't use this indicator in a vacuum. Stocks are a practical foundation for assessing the business cycle, but this foundation needs assistance. Fortunately, there's plenty of assistance available, starting with the primary investment competition for equities: the bond market.

Chapter 4

Straight Talk About Yield Curves

The Treasury market yield curve

U.S. expansions don't die of old age, an economics professor advised in the late-1990s, offering one of the more colorful descriptions of the central bank's influence over the economy. "Every one was murdered by the Federal Reserve," Rudiger Dornbusch insisted.[1] That may be an exaggeration, but it's easy to understand the inspiration behind the indictment: the central bank has a history of raising interest rates just ahead of recessions.

Coincidence? Unlikely. It's fair to say that rate hikes are on the short list of probable murder weapons related to the demise of economic expansions through the years. It may be circumstantial evidence, and there are always other factors to consider. But the historical clues look rather damning if only because this pattern is a recurring offense. The inverted yield curve—short rates above long rates— has a habit of showing up at the crime scene, again and again.

We can debate how much of this is cause and effect, but it's hard to dismiss the persistent record of rising short rates followed by recessions soon after. This much is clear: interest rates rarely rise by accident. Through the Fed's open market operations, the central bank holds sway over the price of money—short rates in particular. Under the central bank's direct control is the Fed funds rate, the rate that banks charge one another for unsecured loans, primarily on an overnight basis. In many respects, this number can be thought of as the most important interest rate for the U.S. economy. Indeed, Fed funds drive almost every other rate to some degree— from the price of home mortgages to how much the U.S. Treasury pays for borrowing from the public when selling government bonds.

Given the import of the Fed funds rate, it's no surprise that sharp increases in this benchmark tend be followed in short order with economic slumps (Figure 4.1). Higher borrowing costs alone may not be the sole cause of recessions, but elevated interest rates are surely a key factor. Every recession since the late-1950s has been preceded by a substantial hike in the Fed funds rate. Granted, not every rate hike leads to a recession. But the potential is always lurking, and so this history lesson resonates.

Prima Facie Evidence

Before we investigate further, let's recognize that the Treasury yield curve is positively sloped most of the time. The "curve" is a reference to yields on government securities across various maturity dates. Interest rates on longer-term Treasuries generally exceed the rates on their shorter-term counterparts. For example, if the yield on a 10-year Treasury Note is 5% while a 3-month Treasury Bill is 1%, the term spread is positive by four percentage points (5% less 1%). The actual numbers vary through time as the market continually reacts to news about the

---

[1] Dornbusch (1997).

economy. But the economic rationale for generally expecting an upwardly sloping curve is informed by the truism that investors demand a premium for lending long. The longer the term of a loan, the higher the rate that a borrower pays... usually.

A higher yield compensates bond owners (lenders) for the extra risk that accompanies longer-term horizons. For U.S. government securities, which enjoy minimal default risk, the main threat is the potential for rising inflation in the future. As a sovereign government, the U.S. can always print more money to pay off its liabilities. There are limits in practice, of course, for a variety of reasons. But for a government that borrows in its own currency, the danger of default is nil, at least in theory. This is no free lunch because there's always uncertainty about what the money will be worth when the government pays you back.[2]

Figure 4.1
Effective Fed Funds rate (monthly)

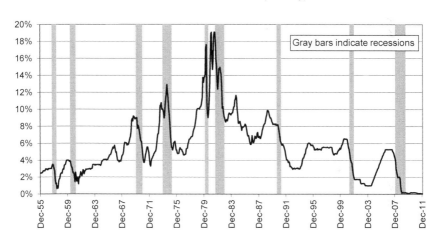

Source: St. Louis Federal Reserve

Over the short term—a year or two—inflation risk is usually quite low for the United States. But looking out 10 or 20 years, well, that requires a greater leap of faith for expecting that the spending power of future coupon payments and the eventual return of principal won't be reduced (or eliminated) through inflation. History offers a guide for assessing this risk, but a certain amount of uncertainty keeps investors guessing in real time. Even if inflation remains contained at a modest

---

[2] There are exceptions to the rule that sovereign governments can always pay off their loans— in particular, consider the European governments in the euro region, where monetary authority has been transferred to a multi-national central bank, the European Central Bank. As such, the authority to "print money" is delegated to the central bank and effectively out of the hands of individual sovereign governments. Also, smaller nations usually enjoy far less flexibility in printing money to pay off liabilities compared with the U.S., which has the advantage of being the world's biggest economy that also issues the world's reserve currency.

level, it still adds up through the years and so the real (inflation-adjusted) return on a bond tends to fall as the investment horizon lengthens.[3]

An entirely different risk scenario applies if deflation—the opposite of inflation—prevails, which translates into higher spending power for a given amount of money. But falling prices on a sustained basis on an economy wide basis is a rare event compared with the historical bias for inflation in the modern era. Accordingly, we should expect low levels of inflation as a general rule in the long run, which implies that long rates will normally exceed short rates.

Figure 4.2
Treasury Yield Curves

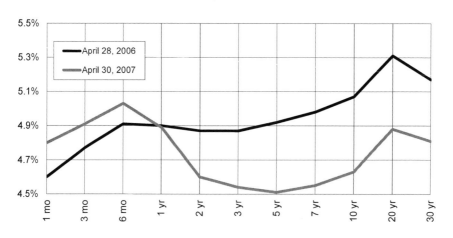

Source: U.S. Treasury

That's the typical relationship, but sometimes the conventional gives way and short rates top long rates. In such periods, history suggests that there's an elevated risk of a new recession in the near future. For example, Figure 4.2 compares the Treasury yield curve on two dates before the start of the 2008-2009 recession. Note that the curve on April 30, 2006 is generally positive, with longer rates rising as maturities lengthen. A year later, April 30, 2007, the curve is inverted: the 3-month Treasury Bill rate of 4.9% exceeds the 10-year Treasury Note's 4.6%, for instance. True to form, a recession arrived soon after—starting in January 2008, according to the National Bureau of Economic Research.

---

[3] I'm referring here and throughout to conventional Treasury securities, which are priced in nominal terms. In contrast, a relative newcomer to the world of government securities is the inflation-indexed Treasury, or TIPS, as these bonds are known. TIPS (Treasury Inflation-Protected Securities) promise to pay real (inflation-adjusted) yields, which effectively eliminates inflation risk, at least in theory, based on the government's proxy for inflation—the Consumer Price Index. As such, TIPS offer the alluring combination of a government security free of inflation and credit risk, or something approximating that ideal. In any case, the discussion in this chapter and for the remainder of the book is focused on conventional (nominal) Treasuries in context with the yield curve.

A key reason (some say the only reason) for the occasional inversion of the yield curve is a change in monetary policy, courtesy of the Federal Reserve. The central bank has a habit of raising short rates after a run of economic growth. Why? It's not the monetary equivalent of sadomasochism, even if feels like it on Main Street. Instead, it's usually an effort to keep a lid on inflation by tightening credit and slowing an expansion that's perceived to be at risk of overheating.

But hiking rates is a blunt tool and it requires a deft central-banking hand to slow the economy and lower inflation without killing the growth trend. Not surprisingly, monetary tightening has a history of going overboard to the point that the cycle succumbs. Actually, that may be the goal, depending on your interpretation of how monetary policy interacts with the real economy.[4]

By design or not, the central bank's attempts at containing or lowering inflation via higher short rates reflects a record of excess, as suggested by the recurring pattern of inverted yield curves and the subsequent economic contractions. A heavy foot on the monetary brakes may be inevitable because of the lagged response time that bedevils policy decisions. Aiming at a moving target is never easy when managing an entire economy. At best, it's monumentally difficult to apply just the right amount of monetary tightening at just the right time and wait months to decide if your choices were helpful or not. Simple human error, it's safe to say, is probably a factor in the connection between policy choices and recessions.

The causes for why, or if, central bank policy goes too far at times need not concern us here. What's relevant is the persistence of the historical relationship between inverted curves and recessions. Numerous studies report that in those rare cases when the term spread moves into negative territory (short rates exceed long rates), the change is associated with restrictive monetary policy, which boosts the odds that a new recession is near. It's fairly obvious what's going on here. If borrowing costs are higher, spending is probably destined to fall, if only on the margins. But sometimes a marginal decline in spending is enough to set off a chain reaction that leads to a recession.

The dynamic nature of market sentiment play a role in changing the shape of the yield curve too. If the crowd senses that there's a recession brewing—perhaps due to rate hikes by the Fed—the demand for safety takes wing. As a result, the inherent security of government bonds offers greater appeal for investors during periods of rising economic anxiety. In turn, that has an effect on the yield curve.

Recall that yield and price are inversely related for fixed-income securities: buying bonds and bidding up prices equates with lower yields. In a period of rising concern about the business cycle, for whatever reason, there's a greater appetite for a safe harbor. The idea of parking money in a guaranteed Treasury bond that provides a secure corner for the near term needs no explanation when there's greater uncertainty about the economic outlook.

Meantime, short-term Treasuries are still at the mercy of the Fed funds rate, including the cash proxies such as 3-month Treasury Bills. The yield on a T-Bill

---

[4] For example, the so-called Phillips curve is said to reflect an inverse connection between the unemployment rate and inflation. As unemployment falls, inflation rises, and vice versa. The Phillips curve is named for the economist William Phillips, who outlined the relationship in the 1950s. Although the concept is widely known, there's been a debate for many years about its validity, in part because historical data don't offer clear support for the relationship.

typically rises in sympathy with the central bank's policy of tighter money. That's in contrast to longer-dated Treasury yields, which tend to be influenced by investor demand and the available supply in the marketplace.

The net result of safe-harbor bond buying and central bank rate hikes on the short end is likely to be an inverted yield curve at some point. Recognizing the macro effects that follow a period when short rates exceed long rates is valuable strategic information, but it's not exactly news at this point. Back in 1991, a pair of economists wrote in *The Journal of Finance* that using the yield curve to predict economic activity "outperforms survey forecasts, both in-sample and out-of-sample."[5] A few years later, one of the authors teamed up with another researcher and concluded that "current monetary policy has a significant influence on the yield curve spread and hence on real activity over the next several quarters." In particular, they found that "a rise in the short rate tends to flatten the yield curve as well as to slow real growth in the near term."[6]

This is hardly a shock at this late date. The inverted curve-recession has been studied and widely confirmed by various economists over the years.[7] "Every recession after the mid-1960s was predicted by a negative slope—an inverted yield curve—within 6 quarters of the impending recession," concluded a 2006 paper in the *Journal of Econometrics*.[8] The rise of short rates above long rates constitutes a "reliable signal of an imminent recession," another research team advised in 2008.[9] Recognizing the curve's forecasting record, the Conference Board decided to use the term spread as a component in its widely cited leading indicator of U.S. business activity. The curve has also been a robust leading indicator of the business cycle in foreign economies.[10] For example, a 2005 study reported that the yield curve has an encouraging record of anticipating economic output in several European countries.[11]

Despite the theoretical and empirical legitimacy associated with this gauge, there's always room for skepticism, particularly when it comes to making forecasts in real time. The period after the Great Recession, which ushered in several years of unusual monetary policy, has raised new questions about the yield curve as a predictor of recessions. Because the Federal Reserve dropped short rates to virtually zero for several years and embraced unconventional forms of monetary policy, some analysts argued that the yield curve had become distorted to the point that its signals are no longer valid, at least not until the return of a "normal" policy stance. Exactly when that point arrives is, of course, wide open for debate, in part because defining a "normal" monetary policy is a gray area.

Meantime, it's safe to assume that the yield curve remains a powerful tool for corroborating (or rejecting) recession warnings dispatched by the stock market and other indicators. In addition to its encouraging track record, the yield curve also

---

[5] Estrella and Hardouvelis (1991), p. 555.

[6] Estrella and Mishkin (1996), p. 1.

[7] For a survey of the yield-curve literature, see Wheelock and Wohar (2009).

[8] Ang, Piazzesi and Wei (2006), p. 360.

[9] Rosenberg and Maurer (2008), p. 1.

[10] See, for example, Bernard and Gerlach (1996), Estrella and Mishkin (1997) and Sensier et al. (2002).

[11] Duarte, et al. (2005).

benefits from the fact that it's easily calculated, transparent, and the data isn't subject to revision. It's also available gratis, on a daily basis (treasury.gov).

As for the choice of maturities for calculating the curve, a veteran analyst who's studied the relations between Treasury yields and the business cycle co-authored a recommendation in 2006 on how to proceed:

> In forecasts of real activity, the most accurate results are obtained by taking the difference between two Treasury yields whose maturities are far apart. At the long end of the curve, the clear choice seems to be a ten-year rate, the longest maturity available in the United States on a consistent basis over a long sample period....
>
> With regard to the short-term rate, earlier research suggests that the three-month Treasury rate, when used in conjunction with the ten-year Treasury rate, provides a reasonable combination of accuracy and robustness in predicting U.S. recessions over long periods.[12]

Like all measures of financial and economic conditions, the yield curve falls short of dispensing error-free signals. And different analysts report slightly different results by using different definitions of the term structure of interest rates. Even if we find a particular set of Treasury maturities that outperform others for certain period, that's no guarantee that the edge will hold up over time.

Perfection, as always, is beyond our grasp. Enhancing our strategic intelligence, on the other hand, is a reasonable goal. With that in mind, let's consider how the term structure has fared as a recession predictor over the last 50 years when using monthly data. Six of the last eight recessions were preceded by an inversion of the Treasury yield curve, based on the monthly spread for the 10-year less three-month rates (Figure 4.3).[13] In other words, two recessions struck without a preceding curve inversion (1957-1958 and 1990). But in both cases, short rates came close to topping long rates, suggesting that the curve was flirting with formal warnings. Perhaps the lesson is that a curve that's flat or near flat should be considered a warning as well as an outright inversion.

---

[12] Estrella and Trubin (2006), p. 3.

[13] Analysts report slightly different results in terms of the yield curve's recession forecasting record due to the use of different interest-rate time series. In Chart 4.3, I calculate the spread based on monthly rate averages for the 10-year Treasury less the 3-month T-Bill. By that definition, the curve didn't invert ahead of the 1990 recession, although it came close. In contrast, using the effective Fed funds rate as the short-term proxy dispatches a clear inversion in late-1989 and early 1990. Separately, the use of average monthly data for judging the yield curve's forecasting powers may appear somewhat arbitrary, although monthly numbers help minimize the short-term noise that comes with looking at daily data. Does the use of different frequencies change the yield curve's recession forecast? Yes, or at least sometimes, albeit at the margins. As noted, the yield curve stopped short of inverting ahead of the 1990-1991 recession via monthly rates (10-year Treasury less 3-month Treasury Bill). By contrast, daily numbers from the St. Louis Fed's database reveal that there were five days when the curve inverted in mid-1989—in advance of the recession that began in July 1990. It's debatable if that constitutes a practical signal. In any case, it's wise to monitor data across multiple frequencies and data sets for a broader perspective for analyzing the economy in real time.

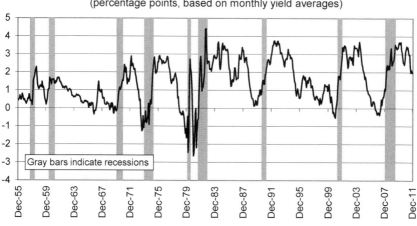

Figure 4.3
Treasury Yield Curve: 10-year Treasury less 3-month Treasury bill
(percentage points, based on monthly yield averages)

Source: St. Louis Federal Reserve

Some analysts are skeptical of looking for deeper clarity by focusing on daily data. One pair of researchers recently warned that "inversions in daily or intraday data often prove to be false signals. Inversions observed over longer periods—at a monthly or quarterly average frequency—provide more reliable signals."[14]

It's worth noting that there was one instance over the past half century when the yield curve inverted without a new recession in due course, based on the monthly data in Figure 4.3. In late-1966 and early 1967, short rates exceeded long rates but it would be nearly three years before the next downturn. To be fair, economic growth slowed considerably after the torrid pace in the first quarter of 1966; the second quarter of 1967 came to a virtual standstill. But if there was a higher risk of recession brewing, it never materialized in the form of official slump, according to NBER.

Imperfect But Practical
The general accuracy of the yield curve's forecasts over the decades is conspicuous. Admittedly, there's no assurance that the term structure of rates will retain its powers of prognostication, but the record strongly suggests that we can't afford to see this

---

[14] Estrella and Trubin (2006), p. 5. They also noted (p. 3) that "maximum accuracy and predictive power are obtained with the secondary market three-month rate expressed on a bond-equivalent basis, rather than the constant maturity rate, which is interpolated from the daily yield curve for Treasury securities." Using data from the Federal Reserve's H.15 release "provides the secondary market rate on a discount basis. To convert the three-month discount rate to a bond-equivalent basis, we apply the transformation: bond-equivalent = 100*(365*discount/100)/(360-91*discount/100), where 'discount' is the discount yield expressed in percentage points." By this definition, all recessions since the late-1960s, including the 1990 recession, were preceded by a negative yield curve, according to Estrella and Trubin.

track record as dumb luck. The fundamental connection between rising short rates and slower economic growth, which can and often does lead to a recession, is a compelling economic narrative that draws on the empirical record, economic theory, and common sense.

As one final piece of evidence, consider how the yield curve has fared as a general rule in advance of the six recessions from 1973 through 2008 (Figure 4.4). As you can see, the term spread for Treasuries has a bias, on average, for turning negative just ahead of recessions since for more than four decades.

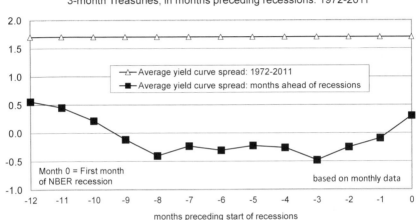

Figure 4.4
Average yield-curve spread, monthly percentage points, 10-year less
3-month Treasuries, in months preceding recessions: 1972-2011

Sources: St. Louis Federal Reserve, NBER, James Picerno

Surprisingly, the yield curve's value as a forward-looking metric has been underutilized if not ignored in some cases—despite the evidence that professional forecasters make their largest errors during recessions.[15] Perhaps that's due to a preference in the dismal science for relatively complicated but not necessarily superior forecasting models born of multi-factor leading indices.[16] At least one study noted the puzzling fact that the yield curve's merits have been known for nearly half a century[17], but forecasters have a history of overlooking the signals.[18]

Popular or not, the task of watching the yield curve can help evaluate the odds of recession risk in context with other sources. Consider the seven false recession signals issued by the stock market since the late-1950s when the 12-month return on the S&P 500 turned negative without a forthcoming recession. Let's filter those misleading warnings through the lens of the yield curve. The result is that six of the

---

[15] See Zarnowitz and Braun (1993), for instance.
[16] See Diebold and Rudebusch (1989, 1991a, and 1991b).
[17] A 1965 NBER study is reportedly the first to identify the yield curve as a business cycle forecasting tool. See Kessel (1965).
[18] Rudebusch and Williams (2009).

seven bogus signals in the equity market were not accompanied by an inverted yield curve. In other words, combining the recession predictions from the U.S. stock market with the yield curve dramatically reduced the false signals dispensed by equities alone.

The weak point remains the warnings in 1966. Both the stock market and the yield curve issued recession signals that year, but the next downturn didn't start until December 1969. Another weak point in the forecasting record for the term spread is the 1990 recession. The stock market anticipated the downturn with a 12-month price loss early in that recession, but the signal wasn't formally confirmed by the yield curve, at least not if we use monthly averages of Treasury rates.[19]

The larger point is that even when combining indicators, we must be aware of the possibility, if not the inevitability, that flawed forecasts can't be fully engineered away. As we'll see in the chapters ahead, adding more indicators to a recession risk model can help reduce the incidence of false signals, but additional variables can also blur the clarity of the analysis if we add too many data sets or rely on indicators of questionable value for business cycle research.

Uncertainty, in short, retains the capacity to surprise. That's hardly an excuse to forgo the combining of indicators from various sources. Using the stock market and the Treasury yield curve is a productive coupling that's stronger than either signal is alone. That's not surprising since each marketplace reflects a different yet relevant aspect of investor sentiment. The clues from Treasuries and equities for assessing the economic outlook, in sum, are generally complimentary.

But this is only the beginning. In the chapters to come, we'll review more than a dozen additional indicators for building a robust measure of recession risk. More is better… up to a point.

Next up: measuring fear by way of the yield spread in high-yield less investment-grade corporate bonds.

---

[19] As discussed above in footnote 14, the Estrella and Trubin (2006) definition of the yield curve did in fact anticipate the 1990 recession.

Chapter 5

The Corporate Connection

Credit spreads

The rationale for expecting a higher yield in low-grade corporate bonds over their high-grade counterparts when the economy is struggling is grounded in common sense as well as theory. If the market anticipates a new recession, it's only natural that investors will seek safer terrain. The net result: risky bonds are sold as the crowd moves into the relatively safe ones. True for government bonds vs. corporates, and true within the corporates arena. One effect is an increase in the credit spread as yields on relatively risky bonds widen in comparison with higher-rated securities.[1]

This particular aspect of the relationship between macro and markets is familiar terrain from a theoretical perspective. The basic narrative is one of fluctuating credit spreads as a reflection of shifting perceptions about default risk, particularly for lesser-rated fixed-income securities. When the economic outlook deteriorates, the market becomes increasingly skeptical about the prospects for the lower tier of debt. Investors therefore demand higher yields as compensation to offset the perceived jump in risk during periods of higher economic vulnerability. Some of this process, perhaps all of it, is set in motion when the central bank increases interest rates to cool an overheating economy. Regardless of the catalyst, the higher cost of financing via elevated rates increases the financial burden on companies if they raise capital in the public markets by selling bonds. In turn, the extra costs borne in the private sector creates one more obstacle for the economy.[2]

You don't have to read the economic literature to see what's obvious from simple observation. The habit of moving to safe or at least safer bonds within the corporate sector is clearly recorded in the historical relationship between the business cycle and the yield difference between high- and low-grade corporates. For example, let's review the evolving spread, as defined by yields for corporate bonds rated Baa by Moody's (the lowest-rated tier of "investment-grade" debt) less the top-rated Aaa group. Unsurprisingly, this spread tends to increase during recessions (Figure 5.1). The timing, however, varies. In January 2008, the first month of the recession, the average credit spread was 1.21 percentage points, up only modestly from previous months. After January 2008, however, the spread rose sharply in rapid fashion, reaching a cyclical peak of 3.38 percentage points by January 2009.[3]

---

[1] Bond yields move inversely with bond prices and so lower bond prices equate with higher yields, and vice versa.

[2] See, for example, Bernanke and Gertler (1995) and Bernanke, et al. (1999). For a broader review of the explanations between credit spreads and the business cycle—as it pertains to the 2008-2009 recession in particular—see Hall (2010), pp. 12-14.

[3] All references here and throughout for corporate yields and spreads are based on monthly averages, unless stated otherwise.

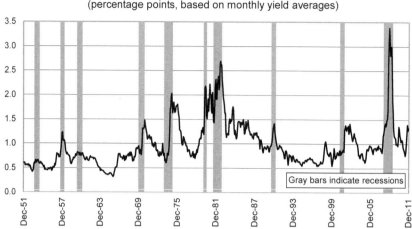

Figure 5.1
Corporate bond yield spread: Moody's Baa yield less Aaa yields
(percentage points, based on monthly yield averages)

Source: St. Louis Federal Reserve

It was another story during the previous downturn. When the short-lived and comparatively mild slump of 2001 commenced in April of that year, the credit spread was less than one percentage point, based on average monthly data. That was slightly higher compared with the preceding months, but as clear and unambiguous signals go this was rather subtle vs. the trend in 2008. In fact, when the 2001 downturn ended in November of that year, the credit spread on average was slightly lower relative to the previous April.

Hazy signals from the credit spread aren't unusual in the search for timely clues about recession risk. As Figure 5.1 reminds, the absolute levels of this spread are unreliable for estimating the odds of a new downturn. Warnings from this indicator usually arrive too late for practical use in real time.

But let's not abandon the credit spread just yet. Looking at the year-over-year percentage changes can be a more useful measure of recession risk (Figure 5.2). Consider the brief 2001 downturn again, this time in terms of the credit spread's annual change. In that case, the spread surged just ahead of the recession's start in April 2001. That's not atypical. Every recession over the last 60 years was accompanied by a credit spread that jumped substantially vs. the year-earlier level relatively early.

Unfortunately, there are still some problems. First, measuring the credit spread by annual changes doesn't always dispatch timely warning signs of an approaching recession. The view from the perspective of yields also brings false positives at times. There have been a number of instances through the decades when the credit spread increased sharply without the onset of a recession in the near term.

Compared with the Treasury yield curve's signals (Chapter 4), the credit spread's record is mixed. Should we abandon this metric for evaluating the business cycle? No, and here's why. Corporate spreads, although imperfect, still impart valuable information about credit conditions—a key factor for profiling the economy. Like every other indicator, this indicator's value waxes and wanes. Much depends on the broader economic backdrop. Credit risk alone doesn't mechanically dictate the economy's path. Sometimes it's relevant, perhaps even decisive, but not always. Unfortunately, it's never clear how or when to distinguish one scenario from the other in advance. But this challenge raises a larger point, and one that deserves a brief discussion before we move on.

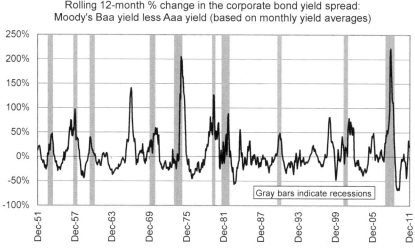

Figure 5.2
Rolling 12-month % change in the corporate bond yield spread:
Moody's Baa yield less Aaa yield (based on monthly yield averages)

Source: St. Louis Federal Reserve

Shades Of (Statistical) Grey

Choosing variables for analyzing the business cycle is ultimately a subjective process. Although it's tempting to think of the broad twists and turns in the economy as one factor, there is no single indicator that consistently and reliably captures the big-picture trend at all times in all conditions. The next best thing is creating a proxy index of multiple indicators that's likely to capture most of what we need to know, most of the time, under multiple scenarios. There are many, many possibilities for constructing such a benchmark. This is at once an opportunity... and a curse.

The primary goal is selecting a representative data set to clarify and explain a specific macro challenge at hand—estimating recession risk, in this case. This can easily turn into a swamp of confusion. The St. Louis Fed's FRED database, for example, offers thousands of data sets that track some aspect of the U.S. economy. How to choose? The obvious starting point is the economic literature. With a grasp of what economists have uncovered over the decades, from both theoretical and empirical perspectives, we can begin to select indicators that further our quest for intelligently developing insight about recession risk.

Along the way, it's important to remember that no one indicator is going to be all things at all times. Actually, let's be fair and recognize that each and every indicator is surely destined to stumble at times. No one knows when one highly priced index will deceive us. Even if we find an indicator with a perfect record, that's hardly a reason to expect that its unblemished history will always define its future.

To take an extreme example, let's say that you've identified a variable (or two or three) that exhibit a perfect or near-perfect record for evaluating recession risk, which in turn convinces you to ignore a dozen other relevant indicators with less-impressive records. It appears that you've improved your model considerably. Maybe, but maybe not. Recession risk isn't usually, if ever, captured by one factor, or even a handful of factors. What's more, the catalysts in one recession may play a minimal role, and perhaps no role at all, in the next downturn. Recessions, in some respects, are unique events, each one arising from the confluence of a particular array of conditions—conditions that never repeat, at least not exactly.

Here's the issue in a nutshell. First, a vast literature in macroeconomics research tells us—screams at us—that we should expect misleading signals from any one indicator, even if the track record suggests otherwise. Actually, a perfect record suggests that the indicator is overdue for leading us astray, given the dynamic nature of the economy. But there's also the reality that no one knows which indicators will shine, or which ones will crumble, in the months and years ahead. There's really no other choice other than carefully selecting a broad, representative sample to minimize the risk that one (or more) seemingly reliable benchmarks could crash and burn the next time.

Flawed But Still Relevant
That brings us back to the credit spread. As a lone metric, its value waxes and wanes for assessing the threat of recession. But that's hardly unusual when looking at individual data series. What's clear is that during those times when the credit spread increases, it's reflecting financial stress of one kind or another.

The presence of financial stress, as reflected in widening credit spreads, contains critical information for evaluating the economy, according to a growing list of empirical studies.[4] Most of this indicator's insight is related to its countercyclical nature vis-a-vis the business cycle. It's no surprise to discover that financial stress tends to rise ahead of and/or during economic recessions. But it's also true—and this is a crucial point—that a rise in financial stress isn't always accompanied by an economic downturn.

Why? Because financial stress is one of many factors that can trigger a recession. Much depends on the broader economic context. Remember that no one really understands the true process that leads to recessions. Even if we could decipher the specific causes of the last recession, it's unlikely that the analysis would bring full clarity for the next one. Every recession is different, which means that the underlying causes evolve. There are common factors, but assuming that the next contraction will emerge for the same reasons in the same way ignores the historical record.

Under the right conditions, elevated financial stress can certainly be a contributing factor for the onset of a recession, perhaps even directly cause it. But history also shows that financial stress alone may not be enough to push an economy

---

[4] For example, see Faust, et al. (2011), Covas and Den Haan (2011), and Gilchrist, et al. (2009).

over the edge. One study, for instance, finds that the credit spread's value as a predictor of economic activity is dependent on "high and volatile" inflation,[5] which may or may not be present.

Another reason why a jump in financial stress isn't always linked with a drop in economic output is because the magnitude of financial shocks varies, as do the underlying macro conditions and an economy's ability to absorb the shocks. A relatively mild financial tremor can be quite disruptive if the economy is already weak. On the other hand, a fairly large financial shock may have a limited impact during a period of robust economic growth.

As one example, the 1997-1998 Asian financial crisis—initially triggered by the dramatic fall in the Thai baht— stirred worries that the global economy would suffer. Although the U.S. was insulated to a degree, the financial markets still reacted. Corporate yield spreads, for instance, widened sharply during a short period— roughly doubling in the U.S. from a monthly average of around 60 basis points in July 1997 (just as the crisis was beginning in Asia) to over 100 basis points by the end of the year and on into early 1998.

The shock wave was evident beyond the corporate fixed-income market. A number of financial stress indices that measure a range of variables, such as capital markets liquidity, foreign exchange rates, stock market volatility, and other items, were also flashing warning signals at the time. The Kansas City Fed Financial Stress Index rose sharply from July 1997 through mid-1998, reaching new highs that year. Similar trends were unfolding in other benchmarks, including the St. Louis Financial Stress Index and the Chicago Fed National Financial Conditions Index.[6]

For all its implied threat, the financial crisis in Asia never infected the real economy in the U.S., at least not enough to derail the general trend and unleash a new recession. A number of key economic indicators reflected continued expansion during the months when the Asian financial upheaval deepened and spread. The U.S. labor market, for example, continued to rise at a healthy clip during this period. Personal income and spending remained buoyant as well, as did industrial production in 1997 and 1998. Recession risk for the U.S., in short, was low in the wake of the Asian financial crisis. The economy's growth momentum was apparently strong enough to withstand even a global financial crisis.

But in those instances when downturns and financial crises do coincide, beware: the macro damage is usually severe. Researchers report that downturns associated with financial crises tend to be deeper and last longer. A series of studies by economists Carmen Reinhart and Kenneth Rogoff document that severe banking and financial crises and recessions aren't exactly strangers. As they explain in a 2009 paper:

> Broadly speaking, financial crises are protracted affairs. More often than not, the aftermath of severe financial crises share three characteristics. *First*, asset market collapses are deep and prolonged. Real housing price declines average 35 percent stretched out over six years, while equity price collapses average 55 percent over a downturn of about three and a half years. *Second*, the aftermath of banking crises is associated with

---

[5] Mody and Taylor (2003), p. 373.
[6] Data available at research.stlouisfed.org.

profound declines in output and employment. The unemployment rate rises an average of 7 percentage points over the down phase of the cycle, which lasts on average over four years. Output falls (from peak to trough) an average of over 9 percent, although the duration of the downturn, averaging roughly two years, is considerably shorter than for unemployment. *Third,* the real value of government debt tends to explode, rising an average of 86 percent in the major post–World War II episodes.[7]

Given this record, it follows that credit spreads "embed crucial information about the one-year-ahead probability of recession." as a recent Federal Reserve study observed.[8] The study, by the way, also noted that the value of credit spreads as a measure of the business cycle is even stronger when combined with the signals from the Treasury yield curve.

The Art And Science Of Combination

The blending of signals from various sources potentially offers the biggest bang for our analytical buck, so to speak. The challenge is clear, as are the stakes. At one extreme, relying on any one signal, regardless of how well it's performed in the past, is setting us up for trouble. Yet combining more indicators has limits too. At some point, adding more indicators to a model won't improve the overall signal, and the additions may very well end up degrading the analytics by introducing more noise into the data.

A certain amount of trial and error is inevitable for testing and selecting variables that move us closer to the competing demands of parsimony and assembling a statistically robust set of indicators that collectively capture the essential features of business cycle fluctuations. Sometimes a worthy candidate may appear to be of minimal value. But that's only one aspect to consider. The other is how the indicator fares in its contribution to the overall signal. That's usually a tougher question to answer, but essential nonetheless. The aggregate signal, based on multiple indicators, is the critical piece of information. Choose wisely, but choose broadly.

Fortunately, we can find guidance in a number of economic studies as well as crunching the numbers independently, with and without credit spreads and other variables. The result, however, is clear: using credit spreads tends to enhance the strategic intelligence for measuring recession risk through time. That's not the same as saying that credit spreads will always dispense timely, relevant and superior information. That's a caveat that also applies to every other indicator. But since we can never be sure of when, or if, a lone indicator will fail us—or when it will dispatch critical information—it's vital that we prudently build a broad data set to 1) minimize the risk of noise; and 2) boost the odds of receiving a rich signal. By that standard, it's easy to see why we can't overlook the yield spread between high- and low-grade corporate debt.

For instance, let's review how the credit spread compares, on average, during the 12 months leading up to start of recessions since the early 1970s (Figure 5.3). As you can see, there's an obvious upward bias in the months leading up to downturns.

---

[7] Reinhart and Rogoff (2009a), p. 3.

[8] King, et al. (2007), p. 1.

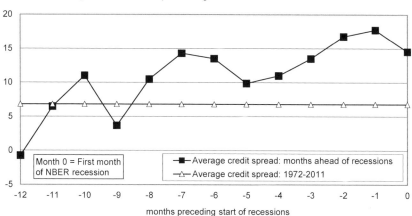

Figure 5.3
Average credit spread, monthly percentage points: Moody's Baa less Aaa
yields, in months preceding the start of recessions: 1972-2011

Sources: St. Louis Federal Reserve, NBER, James Picerno

Finally, let's recognize that there are several credit spreads to consider, and some offer a more-sensitive read on economic conditions than others. One popular choice is the yield spread in Moody's Baa credit less its Aaa counterpart—a pair that's used in the charts above and in the business cycle model outlined at the end of the book. The main reason for using the Moody's data is its long history—nearly a century. A lengthy record is ideal for analysis and building models. But the rise of "junk" bonds (below investment-grade corporate bonds) since the 1980s has introduced a new and potentially more valuable benchmark for calculating credit spreads.

Let's compare the credit spread as computed by junk bonds over Aaa bonds vs. the Baa-Aaa spread that's discussed above. Because the modern history of junk bonds is relatively short, the historical record is limited. But the available numbers suggest that using below-investment grade bonds may deliver a more-sensitive measure of financial conditions, which in turn may offer an earlier warning of rising recession risk. For instance, ahead of the 2001 and 2008-2009 recessions, the junk-bond credit spread rose higher and earlier vs. its Baa-Aaa equivalent (Figure 5.4).

There's no way of knowing if the earlier warning in the previous cycles will prevail in the years ahead. Nonetheless, monitoring junk spreads is likely to be a productive exercise, if only to supplement the Baa-Aaa analysis. A number of studies suggest no less. "The high-yield spread outperforms other leading financial indicators, including the term spread, the paper-bill spread, and the Federal Funds rate," according to a 1999 research paper.[9] A 2010 inquiry also found that the junk-bond spread provides greater forecasting accuracy of jobs growth than the Treasury yield curve and other indicators, albeit based on a relatively short history.[10]

---

[9] Gertler and Lown (1999), p. 132.
[10] Kishor and Koenig (2010),

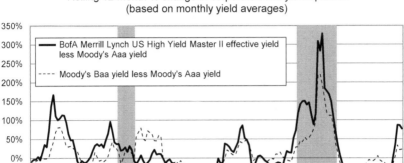

Figure 5.4
Rolling 12-month % change in corporate bond yield spreads
(based on monthly yield averages)

Source: St. Louis Federal Reserve

The main message is that the credit spread is a valuable metric for assessing the business cycle and estimating the potential for recession risk. It's not perfect, but thinking that it would be is just plain naïve. History, however, is clear on at least one point: measuring the shifting state of financial stress is too important to ignore when evaluating the business cycle. Unfortunately, we have no choice but to work with less-than-perfect indicators.

Chapter 6

The Critical Indicator

The labor market

In the search for relevant variables in business cycle analysis, economist Robert Hall once remarked that "the labor market occupies center stage in modern theories of fluctuations. The most important phenomenon to explain and understand in a recession is the sharp decline in employment and jump in unemployment."[1]

Finn Kydland, writing for the Cleveland Federal Reserve a generation ago, burnished the point by estimating that "perhaps on the order of two-thirds of the business cycle is accounted for by movements in the labor input and one-third by changes in technology. Thus, most business-cycle theorists agree that an understanding of aggregate labor-market fluctuations is a prerequisite for understanding how business cycles propagate over time."[2]

Countless studies and investigations of the economy have been published in the two decades since Kydland's observation, but his point still stands. We can debate the specific numbers, but quite a lot of what's generally recognized as the business cycle is bound up with the rise and fall of employment. We can no more minimize, much less dismiss, the labor market in our evaluations of recession risk than we can overlook the sun when studying the solar system.

On many levels, the ebb and flow of the economy's capacity to create jobs is at the core of the broad macro fluctuations that we're trying to model. For theorists, however, integrating this obvious fact into a model that also jibes with the real world on a transparent and practical level is complicated, particularly as it relates to real business cycle theory (RBCT). As we briefly discussed near the end of Chapter 2 and at the start of Chapter 3, the concepts of equilibrium in macroeconomics and the persistence of recessions aren't natural allies. The conflict represents a challenge for using RBCT to explain the economy's recurring bouts of what might be called disequilibrium. Resolving this clash of ideas is a subject that's far beyond the scope of our focus here, which is primarily one of developing a practical methodology for anticipating recessions. We'll leave the task of explaining these loose-end events in a theoretically satisfying manner to others.

Empirically speaking, the basic facts are clear: the economy's power to create jobs suffers during recessions. That's patently obvious, but the crucial issue is deciding if there are early warning signs connected with a deterioration in the employment trend—signs that can tell us that recession risk is rising. Many economists are skeptical. The Conference Board, for example, labels payrolls as a coincident indicator and unemployment levels as a lagging signal—categorizations that reflect a legacy that dates to the pioneering business cycle research from Wesley

---

[1] Hall (1999), p. 1137.
[2] Kydland (1993), p. 1.

Mitchell and Arthur Burns in the late-1930s.[3] In any case, the implication in these labels is that signals from the labor market are of minimal use for evaluating the business cycle in real time. But that's an overly harsh view. The labor market is actually quite useful as a contributing factor for developing a recession-risk warning system. In particular, a range of employment data has proven to be productive:

- Private-sector payrolls (via the Labor Department's Establishment Survey)[4]
- Initial jobless claims (new filings for unemployment benefits)
- The civilian workforce employed-to-unemployed ratio (via the Labor Department's Household Survey).[5]
- The index of aggregate weekly hours worked (private-sector production and nonsupervisory employees)

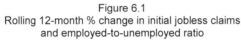

Figure 6.1
Rolling 12-month % change in initial jobless claims
and employed-to-unemployed ratio

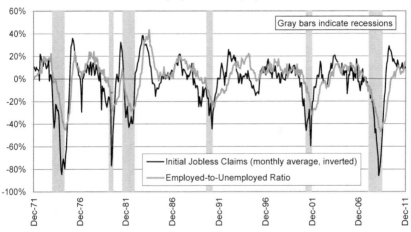

Source: St. Louis Federal Reserve

---

[3] Mitchell and Burns (1938) introduced the concept of leading, coincident, and lagging indicators for business cycle analysis and refined the methodology in Burns and Mitchell (1946).

[4] The U.S. Labor Department also publishes another series of employment data in the so-called Household Survey. The collection methodology differs from the Establishment Survey and so the two series may offer conflicting signals on labor conditions in the short run. But those differences are minimal when compared on a year-over-year basis. As such, the two series are somewhat redundant in terms of annual percentage changes. I focus on the Establishment Survey here and throughout. For evaluating the labor market overall, I use additional metrics for a deeper read on jobs, which includes the Household Survey data for computing the population of employed-to-unemployed ratio, as explained below.

[5] Thanks to Bob Dieli, an economist at nospinforecast.com, for alerting me to this indicator.

I'll discuss the details below, including the rationale for choosing this quartet. First, let's review how these indicators compare with the business cycle through the decades. Figure 6.1 shows the history of initial jobless claims (monthly average, inverted) and the employed-to-unemployed ratio. As you'd expect, both indicators are sensitive to the onset of recessions. The employed-to-unemployed ratio tends to decline relative to its year-earlier levels, either in advance of recessions or during the early months of downturns. A similar relationship is evident with jobless claims and the start of economic slumps (for easier comparison I've inverted the claims data). In other words, rising claims for unemployment benefits—a sign that economic growth is weakening—is another business cycle proxy by way of the labor market.

Figure 6.2 profiles the year-over-year percentage changes for two other labor market indicators: private-sector payrolls and the index of aggregate weekly hours worked for production and nonsupervisory employees. These two data sets also tend to suffer negative comparisons on an annual basis with the approach of recessions.

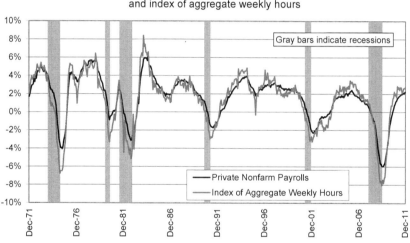

Figure 6.2
Rolling 12-month % change in private nonfarm payrolls
and index of aggregate weekly hours

Source: St. Louis Federal Reserve

Each of the four data series reflects a particular facet of labor market conditions. In the aggregate, this quartet paints a useful profile of the economy's capacity to create jobs. This is a critical issue for analyzing the business cycle. So critical, in fact, that we should go the extra mile to minimize the risk that a given measure of the labor market may be misleading us at any point in time.

One way to manage this risk is by looking to several metrics, each measuring different aspects of the workforce. We can then take an average measure of the indicators and track the resulting year-over-year change. This diversified approach filters out some of the seasonal noise and limits the distortions that can arise in any one indicator. The result is what I'll refer to as the Labor Market Index (LMI), which is shown in Figure 6.3. LMI is an average of averages. To be precise, LMI is the monthly average of the four rolling 12-month percentage changes for the four employment indicators noted above. Overall, LMI boasts a better record of dispensing early warning signals of business cycle risk compared with the individual histories of its constituent indicators. Better, but still not perfect.

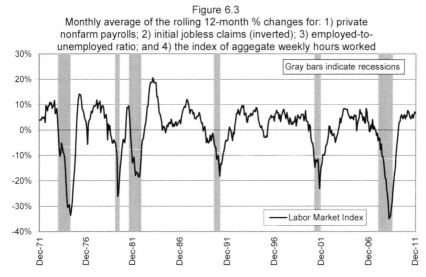

Figure 6.3
Monthly average of the rolling 12-month % changes for: 1) private nonfarm payrolls; 2) initial jobless claims (inverted); 3) employed-to-unemployed ratio; and 4) the index of aggegate weekly hours worked

Source: St. Louis Federal Reserve

As usual when reviewing economic numbers, we shouldn't expect to find an unblemished record in search of metrics that capture the dynamics of macro fluctuations. Indeed, the labor market can and does fluctuate for a variety of reasons, particularly in the short term. Even so, our labor market index in Figure 6.3 has a strong tendency to decline on a year-over-year basis in the early months of the downturn if not just before a recession begins. We can't rely on this benchmark alone, and we're not going to. But it's clear that this index of four inputs performs a generally reliable job of capturing the primary trend for labor market conditions.

A picture's worth a thousand words on this point, as the next chart shows. Indeed, history reminds that the labor market generally deteriorates just ahead of the business cycle's peak. Any one moment in time may or may not conform to this pattern, but the trend is clear (Figure 6.4). For the decades 1972 through 2011, the Labor Market Index (LMI) has a bias for a sharp and relatively sudden declines on an annual basis just as the economy is close to peaking. Once the first month of recession kicks in, LMI is apt to reflect a loss vs. its year-earlier level.

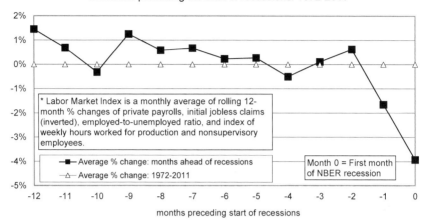

Figure 6.4
Average % change of Labor Market Index*
in months preceding the start of recessions: 1972-2011

* Labor Market Index is a monthly average of rolling 12-month % changes of private payrolls, initial jobless claims (inverted), employed-to-unemployed ratio, and index of weekly hours worked for production and nonsupervisory employees.

Average % change: months ahead of recessions
Average % change: 1972-2011

Month 0 = First month of NBER recession

months preceding start of recessions

Sources: St. Louis Federal Reserve, NBER, James Picerno

Even a robust measure of the employment trend can only tell us so much, which is why it's essential to review LMI in context with other indicators. But as lone metrics go in the dark art of dissecting the business cycle, the changing conditions in the economy's ability to produce jobs is an essential tool. We can boil it down to one cardinal principal: The odds are comparatively low that a new recession is near if the labor market's growing.

Chapter 7

A "Fundamental Psychological Law"

Consumer spending

The primary source of economic growth in the U.S. flows from the consumer. We've heard this statement many times—so many times, in fact, that it's tempting to dismiss the observation as cliché. But this cliché happens to be true. Consumers really do drive economic activity in the U.S. That's not necessarily true for every country, although consumer-oriented economies tend to dominate in the industrialized world, and a number of so-called emerging economies are moving in that direction too.

The U.S. is somewhat of an extreme case—no other economy relies so extensively on personal consumption expenditures. For good or ill, that's reality and so any review of the American business cycle must take consumer spending into account. A simple review of gross domestic product (GDP) data tells us why. Consumer purchases in 2011, for instance, comprised 71% of the U.S. economic output, as defined by GDP.[1] Consumer spending has also increased at a slightly faster pace than the economy overall in recent years. For the decade through the end of 2011, real personal consumption expenditures advanced by roughly 1.8% a year, or slightly faster than the 1.7% growth for real GDP, using quarterly data.[2] Before the Great Recession of 2008-2009, consumption's pace over GDP was even higher.

A lot has changed since the economy was brutalized in 2008-2009, of course. Some economists predict that consumer spending will fade as a source of growth for the U.S. in the years ahead.[3] But even if the forecast is accurate, consumer spending will remain the single-biggest piece of GDP for many years to come. Diminished relative to its glory days, perhaps, but dominant nonetheless. The business cycle, in short, will remain closely linked to, and heavily dependent on, the general public's willingness (and capacity) to spend.

That doesn't mean that the consumer is the only relevant factor. Economic indicators that represent a small slice of GDP are sometimes highly relevant in terms of creating trouble for the business cycle. Recessions don't always start within the consumer sphere, but the fallout eventually shows up in personal spending and income data.

That said, the relationship between consumers and the business cycle is hardly static. History once again offers clues for what to expect. Some economic downturns have witnessed sharply lower consumption levels, but not always. In the 2001

---

[1] In nominal dollar terms, according to the U.S. Bureau of Economics, based on data published as of October 2012. The comparable share of personal consumption expenditures relative to GDP in 2011 in real (inflation-adjusted) terms was also 71%.
[2] Using quarterly data via St. Louis Federal Reserve's FRED data base (research.stlouisfed.org), based on the time series PCECC96 (real personal consumption expenditures) and GDPC96 (real GDP), as of October 2012.
[3] Emmons (2012), for example, predicted that "consumer spending will recede as the main engine of U.S. economic growth…" for the foreseeable future.

recession, real personal consumption expenditures (RPCE) slowed but never declined in year-over-year terms. By contrast, one-year changes for RPCE went negative for a time during each of the four recessions through 1990-91, a pattern that repeated during the Great Recession of 2008-2009. The brief 2001 downturn is an exception.

Spending Habits

No one's sure how far consumption will fall (if at all) in future recessions. But economic theory tells us to expect the annual growth of consumer spending to weaken if not decline just ahead of or during the early months of downturns. The reasoning starts with the empirical framework known as the marginal propensity to consume (MPC), which is grounded in common sense: Higher income juices the ability to spend. As Keynes observed long ago, "the amount of aggregate consumption mainly depends on the amount of aggregate income...." He labeled it a "fundamental psychological law... that men are disposed, as a rule and on the average, to increase their consumption as their income increases...."[4]

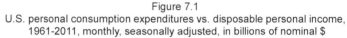

Figure 7.1
U.S. personal consumption expenditures vs. disposable personal income,
1961-2011, monthly, seasonally adjusted, in billions of nominal $

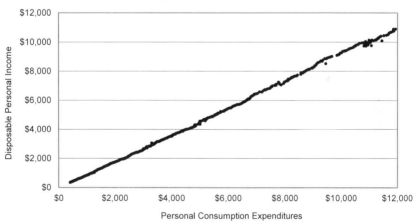

Source: St. Louis Federal Reserve

The data show exactly that, and in starkly clear terms. Few empirical facts in economics are as conspicuous as the positive relationship between spending and income (Figure 7.1). For half a century through 2011, the connection between personal consumption expenditures and disposable personal income has been strong, positive, and consistent. Higher income, in short, is tightly linked with higher spending.

"There are just two things you can do with your income—you either spend it or save it," reminded Bernard Baumohl of the Economic Outlook Group.

---

[4] Keynes [1936] 1964, p. 96.

"Traditionally, the average household spends about 95 percent of every dollar received, and this high level of consumption fuels two-thirds of all economic activity."[5]

Because the connection is so strong and durable, it's reasonable to expect that a decline in income will bring a similar change for spending fairly quickly. In fact, that's generally how economic history has played out. Figure 7.2 compares 12-month percentage changes for real consumer spending and income (less current transfer receipts).[6] It's no surprise that the two indicators track one another fairly closely through time. There are periodic divergences, but it's never wise to assume that spending can rise for very long without a commensurate jump in income.

Note too that income and spending tend to weaken around recessionary periods. That's no surprise either, which tells us why tracking these indicators is useful for monitoring an approaching macro storm. Economist Richard Yamarone summarized the point in *The Trader's Guide to Key Economic Indicators*: "Strong spending is a sign of an expansionary climate; slower spending signals softer economic conditions."[7]

Figure 7.2
Rolling 12-month % change in real consumer spending*
and real personal income less current transfer receipts

Source: St. Louis Federal Reserve

Defining Consumption
Consumer spending in Figure 7.2 (and for the business cycle analysis that follows) is defined by two data sets in real (inflation-adjusted) terms: retail sales and personal

---

[5] Baumohl (2008), p. 64.
[6] Personal current transfer receipts are benefits paid to individuals by government and businesses. Examples include retirement, medical, and disability payments. Because these payments are largely immune to the business cycle, it's essential to measure income without these "transfer receipts" for purposes of analyzing fluctuations in recession risk.
[7] Yamarone (2004), p. 209.

consumption expenditures (PCE). Each has its own set of pros and cons and so averaging the changes for this pair by way of 12-month percentage fluctuations captures a robust sample of consumer spending habits while minimizing some of the short-term noise that can infect these indicators from time to time. For example, retail sales—the main contributor to the broader measure of spending, as defined by PCE—is more sensitive to cyclical fluctuations in the short term. That can be useful to the extent that retail sales respond relatively quickly to consumer distress born of a weaker economy. But the line between cyclical sensitivity and short-term noise can be fuzzy in real time, and so there are limits to using retail sales alone as a proxy for consumer spending.

PCE, as noted, is a broader measure of consumption, and so it tends to be less volatile than retail sales. That can be valuable if we're wary of short-term distortions in our analytical travels. But timeliness is a factor too and PCE has some drawbacks on this front. The monthly PCE updates are published about two weeks after the release of retail sales data.

Nonetheless, the two indicators are intimately related. PCE measures a wider array of spending activity, which means that retail sales are a subset of PCE. "Personal consumption expenditures are derived partly from the Census Bureau's retail sales report, although a significant number of additional sources also provide input," explained Evelina Tainer in *Using Economic Indicators to Improve Investment Analysis*.[8] Indeed, retail sales reflect spending on goods—appliances, cars, food, etc. But that leaves out expenditures on services—everything from haircuts to airline travel. That's a rather big hole when you consider that services account for more than half of all consumer spending. In 2011, for example, consumption of services represented nearly 55% of PCE, according to the U.S. Bureau of Economic Analysis.

A broader read on consumption has its advantages, but so does the narrower measure of spending via retail sales. That's why it's reasonable to take an average of both series (annual percentage changes), a focus that offers an encouraging record for tracking recession risk (Figure 7.2).

Note, however, that the warning signal for spending tends to be a falling rate of growth in the months leading up to an economic slump as opposed to an outright decline. This track record since the early 1970s suggests that consumer expenditures overall will be flat to slightly negative on an annual basis when a recession begins (Figure 7.3).

The history that shows the growth rate of aggregate spending tends to slow rather than decline is a reminder that consumption rolls on, even during recessions. Although discretionary expenditures are vulnerable, people still need to buy groceries, put gas in their cars, heat their homes in the winter, and engage in a variety of activities that are somewhat resistant to the darker shades of the business cycle. Nonetheless, it's clear that the national level of consumption slows to a crawl when the economy deteriorates. Vacations can be delayed, a new car can wait, and junior doesn't really need a new smart phone with all the trimmings after all.

The inspiration for squeezing discretionary spending is directly tied to headwinds for income growth. As jobs become tougher to find and layoffs increase, disposable

---

[8] Tainer (2006), p. 66.

income suffers, which invariably pinches spending. This recurring pattern through time is a valuable input in our search for clues that recession risk is rising.

We can't rely on consumer spending data alone for analyzing the business cycle, but neither can we ignore this piece of the economy and expect to generate robust estimates of recession risk.

Figure 7.3
Average 1-year % change for Consumer Spending Index*,
in months preceding the start of recessions: 1972-2011

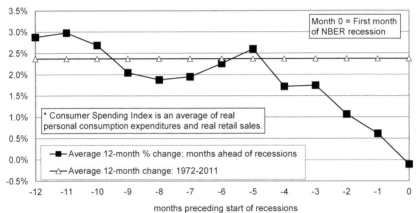

months preceding start of recessions

Sources: St. Louis Federal Reserve, NBER, James Picerno

Sentimental Data

Let's bring in another perspective that compliments the hard data on spending and income via a measure of sentiment, otherwise known as consumer expectations. James Wilcox, a professor at the Haas School of Business at the University of California, Berkeley, explained that measuring consumer attitudes can shed light on current as well as expected economic conditions.[9] Surveys of this type are thought to capture information that's not reflected in conventional economic statistics, according to Wilcox.

In fact, a number of studies report that consumer confidence measures are helpful for projecting spending habits.[10] A 1995 analysis in *Economic Inquiry* estimated that consumer sentiment accounts for about one-fifth of GDP volatility. "The pattern is striking," according to the authors. "All recessions were preceded by a fall in confidence, and all major falls in consumer sentiment were followed by a recession (except in 1965 which, while not a recession, was the so-called 'growth recession'). Apparently either consumers were correctly forecasting output falls, or declines in consumer sentiment were inducing declines in output." [11]

---

[9] Wilcox (2008).
[10] For example, see Fuhrer (1988), Carroll, et al. (1994), and Bram and Ludvigson (1998).
[11] Matsusaka and Sbordone (1995), p. 296.

Updating the numbers in the 21st century doesn't change the pattern. As Figure 7.4 shows, consumer sentiment weakened ahead of the 2000 and 2008-2009 recessions, based on rolling 12-month-percentage-change comparisons for the Reuters/University of Michigan Consumer Sentiment Index. But it's also true that sentiment sometimes falls relative to its year-earlier level without a broad-based downturn that follows in due course. As usual, perfection eludes any one data set as a real-world guide for monitoring the business cycle.

Figure 7.4
Rolling 12-month % change: Reuters/University of Michigan
Consumer Sentiment Index** vs. Consumer Spending Index*

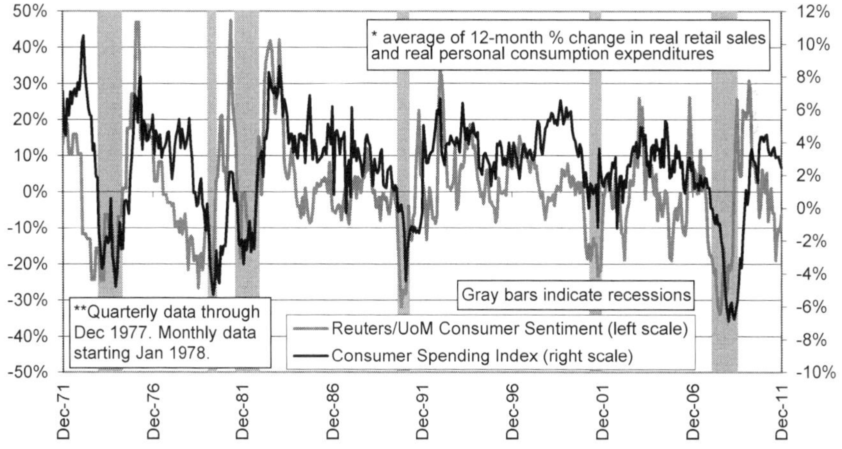

Source: St. Louis Federal Reserve

Does this imperfect history conflict with the observation in the 1995 study noted above that economic contractions followed "all major falls in consumer sentiment"? Not necessarily, since the definition of "major" declines is open for debate. A decrease on a rolling one-year basis is a reasonable proxy for "major." But let's not fool ourselves here. It's clear that sentiment alone can't be counted on as a reliable warning system. That's not a problem, however, since there's no reason why we must rely exclusively on this (or any other) metric for analyzing business cycle risk.

The question is whether consumer sentiment brings another perspective to our quest to uncover deeper strategic intelligence? History suggests answering with a cautious "yes." Sometimes a retreat in consumer spending is a leading trigger of recession, but not always. When consumption is a catalyst, however, sentiment can provide an early clue that trouble's brewing, perhaps in advance of signals based on the spending data proper. Consider how consumer expenditures and sentiment played out in the months leading into the 2008-2009 recession. For a more realistic analysis of the available data at the time, let's review so-called vintage numbers—the data as initially reported, before any revisions.[12]

Figure 7.5 shows that the vintage 12-month percentage changes for consumer spending (real retail sales and real personal consumption expenditures) warned of the mounting cyclical risk in relatively subtle terms. For example, in the last month of the expansion (December 2007), real retail sales dropped by a comparatively mild 0.6% vs. the year-earlier level. But real personal consumption expenditures were still higher by 1.5% on a year-over-year basis on the eve of the Great Recession. The Reuters/University of Michigan Consumer Sentiment Index, by contrast, was clearly warning us at the time that trouble was brewing. When the business cycle peaked (December 2007), this measure of the mood on Main Street had already been posting several months of fairly steep annual declines.

Figure 7.5
Rolling 12-month % change: Reuters/University of Michigan Consumer
Sentiment Index vs. consumer spending (all data is vintage)

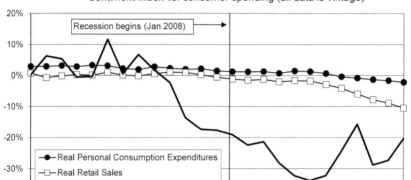

Source: St. Louis Fed

Sentiment doesn't always provide such distinctive early warnings and so it's important to emphasize that the history in Figure 7.5 may not apply the next time. Even when the mood does deteriorate, there's the challenge of deciding if a sharp tumble is a genuine danger sign of impending recession risk vs. a reflection of other concerns that are less threatening to the broad economic trend. Actually, that's a problem that bedevils every indicator at times, which is why it's essential to monitor a wide array of data as a defense.

A warning that arises from a carefully selected set of economic and financial indicators is less likely delude us compared to an alert from one or two variables. On

---

[12] I'll discuss vintage data in more detail in chapters 12 and 13. Meantime, keep in mind that consumer sentiment data, although subject to revisions, tends to undergo fewer and less dramatic changes compared with retail sales and personal consumption expenditures.

that score, consumer sentiment helps us diversify our analysis because it captures a different facet of the economic trend as it relates to current and future spending habits. This is hardly a replacement for actual spending and income metrics, but it's a valuable compliment.

The reasoning, as Bernard Baumohl explained, is based on a belief "that while it's virtually impossible to predict consumer behavior with any precision, Americans do seem more adept at picking up early signs of an economy that is starting to sputter than they are at identifying the beginning of a recovery." Why? One theory, according to Baumohl, is that "households are more acutely sensitive to losing money than gaining it."[13]

---

[13] Baumohl (2008), p. 97.

Chapter 8

Corporate America

Industrial production, real manufacturing & trade sales, and
ISM manufacturing and ISM non-manufacturing (services) indexes

In the previous chapters we've seen that the business cycle, although unobservable directly, is recognizable through a variety of indicators. The financial markets, the labor market, and consumer spending and income habits exhibit cyclical variation that's useful for estimating recession risk. Now we turn to commerce and for a rather obvious reason: business activity tends to weaken directly ahead of, or during the early stages, of economic contractions. As a result, the business sector provides yet another dimension of the macro realm to track for an early warning of cyclical trouble.

On first pass, it appears that the contribution to the U.S. economy from commercial entities is minimal and therefore irrelevant. As a percentage of the nation's output, corporate America's relevance surely pales next to the consumer sector. Whereas personal consumption expenditures in recent years have accounted for around 70% of gross domestic product (GDP), private nonresidential fixed investment linked to businesses—a measure of commercial spending on everything from plants and equipment to computers and software—weighs in at a comparatively slight 12%.[1]

Yet businesses are just as sensitive, if not more so, to economic deterioration as the consumer sector. If companies believe that spending for their products and services will decline in the foreseeable future, corporate chieftains may reason that it's timely to downshift production and generally slow or reduce investment in plants, labor, real estate, etc. As economist Evelina Tainer observed:

> Investment spending reflects only about one-sixth of GDP. However, changes in investment spending, which are significant, exacerbate the business cycle. Growth in investment expenditures outpaces GDP growth during cyclical upswings, while declines outpace GDP contractions.[2]

Spending by companies is one way to monitor the pulse of business activity; another is watching production levels. Why not focus on GDP? After all, this is the broadest measure of the nation's output and so this benchmark captures the broad trends in business activity. But GDP suffers from a long lag time and a quarterly frequency. Fortunately, there are superior metrics for evaluating the changing winds in the commercial sector on a timely basis.

One is industrial production, the granddaddy of U.S. economic data series. Devised by the Federal Reserve around the time of the central bank's founding in 1913, the monthly index of industrial output is pro-cyclical, according to economist

---

[1] Based on real (inflation-adjusted) dollars for 2011, according to the U.S. Bureau of Economic Analysis.
[2] Tainer (2006), p. 87.

Richard Yamarone. "It moves in unison with the business cycle."[3] Casual observation provides confirmation, particularly when reviewing year-over-year changes in the index.

The explanation for why industrial production is a key variable for monitoring and measuring the business cycle is no less transparent. As a gauge of the broad output of manufacturing, mining and utility sectors, industrial activity serves as a rough proxy for gross domestic product (GDP). Its value as an economic indicator is all the more useful when used in context with other measures of output in the commercial sector. For example, consider how one-year percentage changes for industrial production compare with real manufacturing and wholesale trade sales in recent decades (Figure 8.1). Although each series goes its own way at times, in the months leading up to a recession, and after the contraction begins, there's a clear decline in both indicators on a year-over-year basis. In fact, quite a lot of the time the two data sets are virtually indistinguishable from one another when measured in annual percentage terms.

Figure 8.1
Rolling 12-month % change in real manufacturing & wholesale trade sales and industrial production

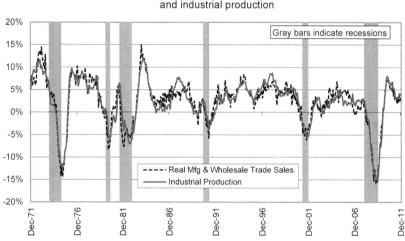

Source: St. Louis Federal Reserve

Both indicators track commercial activity, but they're complimentary as a pair. Industrial production quantifies the total output of manufacturers, mining companies, and utilities. As such, this index reflects real activity as opposed to dollar-value estimates of production. A 10% decline in the industrial production index, for example, equates with a 10% fall in the volume of output. The use here as it relates to the business cycle is that if the nation's industrial sector is slowing, the economy overall is at risk of a slowdown or worse.

---

[3] Yamarone (2004), p. 95.

Manufacturing and wholesale trade sales (MWTS) also track businesses in the economy, but the emphasis with this measure is on sales rather than production quantities. The inflation-adjusted data for MWTS provides a comprehensive measure of a critical factor for all commercial enterprises: revenue. The economy is vulnerable if the real dollar value of sales is falling on a year-over-year basis across a broad range of industries for any length of time.

Looking at both indicators together offers a deeper read on how the business sector overall is faring. In particular, if industrial production and MWTS are trending lower—particularly if they're falling relative to year-earlier levels—that's a forceful signal for thinking that economic growth is weakening.

Two additional resources for taking pulse of the corporate world are the sentiment surveys among so-called purchasing and supply managers in the manufacturing and services sectors, as published by the Institute for Supply Management, a non-profit group that releases monthly updates. The surveys are based on executives from around the country, asking their views on several aspects of business activity. The composite index aggregates the responses across five topics: new orders, production, employment, supplier deliveries, and inventories.

The results from the completed questionnaires sent to managers each month are divided into positive, negative and neutral categories. In turn, the answers are transformed into what's known as a diffusion index. The ISM applies a straightforward calculation to determine if the overall results are higher, lower, or unchanged vs. the previous month. The index values range from zero to 100, with values over 50 associated with economic growth; below-50 readings equate with contraction.

The older of the two series—the ISM Purchasing Managers (PMI) Index for the manufacturing sector—dates to 1948. Through time, manufacturing has come to represent a falling share of the economy in terms of the dollar value. Nonetheless, manufacturers tend to be more sensitive to the business cycle, even if they're using more technology and fewer workers to produce more products.

Meantime, the U.S. economy has increasingly become dominated by services firms through the years. Although the industries in this sector aren't as sensitive to the business cycle compared with manufacturers, it's folly to ignore the vast landscape of commercial enterprise that falls under the general heading of services.

The ISM Non-Manufacturing Composite Index that tracks the services sector is a relatively new indicator, with data starting in 2008. A related measure, the ISM Non-Manufacturing Business Activity Index, goes back a bit further, to 1997. Meanwhile, the calculation details for the services surveys are slightly different from the manufacturing series, although the basic premise is the same: asking opinions of purchasing and supply managers from a variety of industries, such as real estate and banking, entertainment and healthcare. In other words, industries that don't fall under the general heading of manufacturing.

The key point here is that the ISM surveys provide another perspective on the commercial sector. Whereas industrial production tracks output and MWTS measures the dollar value of sales, the ISM benchmarks quantify the mood among business managers. Unsurprisingly, sentiment in the commercial world tends to deteriorate in advance of recessions, as shown in Figure 8.2.

Figure 8.2
% above/below neutral reading of 50: ISM Composite Manufacturing Index
and ISM Non-Manufacturing Composite Index

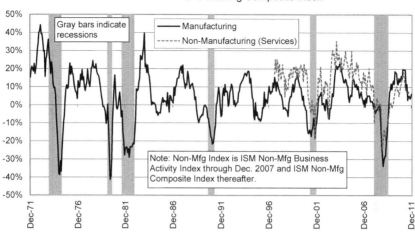

Source: St. Louis Federal Reserve

This is a good time to review the design parameters of the ISM indexes, which influences how we'll use the data for analyzing business cycle risk. The responses from managers to a series of questions about the state of business conditions are divided into three categories: positive, negative, and neutral. Aggregating the opinions provides the raw material for calculating the indexes so that readings above 50 are considered a signal of economic expansion while below-50 readings equate with contraction. Accordingly, it's best to read the ISM data as presented. In contrast with most of the other data sets explored in this book, I refrain from analyzing the ISM indexes on a year-over-year basis. Instead, Chart 8.2 transforms the readings into percentage differences above or below 50 on a monthly basis.

As you can see, negative percentage readings for a given month tend to be associated with recessions—but not always. The collective outlook and assessment of the business community can and does turn negative for reasons that aren't always relevant for broad macroeconomic analysis that's focused on assessing recession risk. The problem is that it's not usually obvious when the negative signals are relevant, at least when it comes to real-time analysis. A similar challenge harasses ever other indicator as well, as we've been discussing.

The solution is to monitor a portfolio of indicators, each focused on a different aspect of the economy. In the aggregate, the signals provide a rich source of intelligence about the business cycle, even if some of the indicators aren't useful at certain periods. That's certainly true for the ISM indexes. Most of the time there's a connection between negative readings for these sentiment benchmarks and elevated recession risk, and so these indicators are a valuable addition to our analytical arsenal. But sometimes the ISM data issues misleading signals. Fortunately, we can look to other data sets for context.

Indeed, analyzing the ISM in relation with other economic and financial indicators enhances our ability to measure the overall trend. As Koenig (2002) observed, the purchasing managers survey has a long history of high correlation with monetary policy decisions, which also imparts useful information about the business cycle (we'll discuss monetary policy in Chapter 10). No wonder that analysts find the ISM data productive for a range of econometric chores, including estimating the near-term output for the economy overall.[4] A 2012 study reported that the ISM data is "a useful predictor of the direction of change in [industrial production], particularly in the recent decade" and so this manufacturing sentiment index "may provide valuable information about the qualitative conditions of the economy such as the acceleration and deceleration of economic activity."[5]

Indeed, the ISM data are independent of the official government statistics that track conditions in the business sector. The ISM numbers are also qualitatively different in design from the conventional gauges of sales and output. As a result, the ISM's sentiment readings are a constructive compliment to industrial production and commercial sales data. In turn, analyzing all the data sets together affords an informative and robust assessment of the commercial sector's economic trend—a relatively holistic view that's considerably more reliable than any one indicator.

---

[4] Lahiri and Monokroussos (2011), for example, report favorably on using ISM data to "nowcast" U.S. GDP. For additional analysis of ISM benchmarks in a macroeconomic context in recent history, see Bachman (2010).

[5] Tsuchiya (2012). First quote: p. 1302; second quote: p. 1303.

Chapter 9

Energy prices and the business cycle

Crude oil

Oil is the world's most important economic commodity, and it's no slouch when it comes to analyzing the business cycle either. It's not hard to understand why. As the critical input for a wide range of energy products, starting with gasoline, there's a natural and obvious connection between economic activity and the price of a barrel of crude oil. Although the precise nature and the degree of the connection is hotly debated among economists, there's a general consensus that oil is on the short list of factors to monitor for estimating recession risk.

Higher prices aren't always a dark sign for the economy, nor are lower energy costs a reliable signal that a run of stronger growth is just around the corner. Much depends on the broader macro context. But history suggests that we should watch oil prices as one of several influential factors that drive the business cycle. Certainly the most cyclically sensitive corners of the economy are vulnerable to sharply higher oil prices—a vulnerability that has been known to infect the wider economy at times. As one academic investigation discovered after analyzing the connection between energy prices and manufacturing jobs between 1972 and 1988, "oil shocks account for 20–25 percent of the variability in employment growth, twice as much as monetary shocks."[1]

There are several economic explanations that find a key role for crude's influence on economic outcomes. But the basic narrative reduces down to the empirical observation that world GDP growth and global oil production tend to be positively correlated.[2]

That simple fact easily leads to the view that economic growth is at least partly dependent on the supply of oil, which in turn is largely a function of price. Meanwhile, a recent study estimated that the annual changes in U.S. GDP and oil consumption are positively linked, sharing a correlation of 0.50 for the years 1978 through 2008.[3] The relationship, according to Murphy and Hall (2011), implies "the hypothesis that higher oil prices and lower oil consumption are indicative of recessions."[4]

It all looks fairly obvious from a casual perspective, yet the economics literature overall is mixed on the question of causality between economic growth and energy

---

[1] Davis and Haltiwanger (2001), p. 465.

[2] For example, Hirsch (2008) documented a positive correlation between growth rates in the global economy and oil production for 1986 through 2005.

[3] Murphy and Hall (2011), p. 54. Correlations range from -1.0 (perfect negative correlation) to zero (no correlation) to 1.0 (perfect positive correlation). The closer a correlation reading is to 1.0, the stronger the presumed link between the two variables. An earlier study (Hamilton, 1983) also documented statistically significant evidence that oil shocks are a cause, though not necessarily the only one, of changes in the business cycle, namely, the onset of recessions.

[4] p. 55.

consumption. That's not surprising once you recognize that studying different time periods with competing models will yield varying results.[5]

Econometric details aside, a straight review of history reminds that it's naïve to assume that higher oil prices automatically bring a new recession in the near term. A more economically satisfying narrative, as one recent study advised, is to see the relationship of oil prices and the economy as evolving through time.[6]

Nonetheless, the incidence of recessions with relatively high energy prices is sufficiently frequent in the historical record to warrant skepticism that the economy is immune to spikes in oil. Even so, the details surely matter. An increase in oil prices due to a *supply* shock vs. a *demand* shock, for instance, may carry different macro implications, depending on current conditions. In other words, prices that rise due to a sudden drop in supply for, say, geopolitical reasons shouldn't be confused with higher prices born of faster economic growth.

Some analysts emphasize that alternative energy sources are a growing part of the mix for generating electricity, powering vehicles, heating homes and offices, and so on. Meanwhile, the renaissance in US production in recent years inspires predictions that the American economy will soon become invulnerable to the energy challenges that have occasionally caused trouble for the business cycle in decades past. These and related narratives suggest that oil's traditional role is fading as it relates to economic fluctuations. It's an intriguing idea, but one that's premature. Fossil fuels, starting with oil, will remain a critical input for the global economy, and that's not likely to change dramatically, at least not in the near term. In turn, we still can't afford to ignore crude prices as part of a comprehensive strategy for monitoring recession risk.

Environmental and supply worries are on the rise, too, pushing the world to search for more efficient, cleaner forms of fuel. But as energy expert and author Daniel Yergin noted in his 2011 book *The Quest: Energy Security and the Remaking of the Modern World*, "most forecasts show that much of what will be the much larger energy needs two decades from now—75 to 80 percent—are currently on track to be met as they are today, from oil, gas, and coal, although used more efficiently."[7]

Renewables will undoubtedly become a steadily larger piece of the energy mix in the years ahead. But the transition from burning hydrocarbons to solar, wind and other non-fossil fuels will be a slow process. Oil, as a result, will continue to play a central role in the economy, which means that oil prices will remain a key factor for assessing the business cycle.

It's certainly hard to ignore the magnitude of oil's economic footprint. In 2011, for instance, the world consumed a bit more than 88 million barrels of crude per day, worth nearly $3.6 trillion over the course of the year. That's worth nearly one-quarter of the U.S. economy's output, based on gross domestic product.[8]

---

[5] For a review of the literature that's focused on energy consumption and economic growth, see Belke, et al. (2011). For a summary of research on oil prices and economic activity, see Kim (2012).

[6] Blanchard and Gali (2009).

[7] Yergin (2011), p. 5

[8] Based on the following data: an average 88.304 million barrels a day of oil consumed, at an average annual price of $111.26 in 2011, according to data from U.S. Energy Information Administration and the U.S. Bureau of Economic Analysis.

The Modern Age Of Oil Volatility

Recognition that fluctuations in crude's price can play a prominent role in the business cycle became obvious rather suddenly in late-1973 and early 1974, when the modern age of energy economics burst onto the world stage in a new and threatening way. The oil-rich oil nations in the Middle East, proclaiming support for the Arab attack on Israel in October 1973, announced an oil embargo soon after the hostilities started. The focus of the embargo: the United States, which supplied Israel with weapons and moral support. The Arab-dominated Organization of the Petroleum Exporting Countries, or OPEC, deployed the oil weapon 10 days after Syria and Egypt launched their surprise attacks on Israel. OPEC announced on October 16, 1973 that it was raising the price on crude by 70%.[9]

Henry Kissinger recalled years later that "the October 16 OPEC decision on price, the October 17 Kuwait decision on Arab production cutbacks, and the October 20 Arab embargo together revolutionized the world oil market." But the "true impact of the embargo was psychological," he reasoned. "The fear that it might be extended—that Arab production might shut down further—triggered a wave of panic buying by Europe and Japan, which constricted supplies and drove prices up even more."[10]

Given the speed and magnitude of the price increase, it's no accident that the U.S. economy quickly fell into recession. Prior to the embargo, low oil prices and abundant supply had been the norm for years. Virtually overnight, the energy outlook turned chaotic and uncertain with the realization that the country's economic future was at the mercy of foreign suppliers with unforgiving anti-American perspectives.

As for the state of macro affairs in 1973 ahead of the oil crisis, one question that arises today: Was a recession destiny even if energy prices had remained stable? It's impossible to know, although it's clear that the economy's vulnerabilities at the time were exacerbated by an unprecedented energy shock. The downturn that began in December 1973 and lasted through March 1975 was the country's deepest and longest economic contraction, up to that point, since the Great Depression.

In looking for a broader lesson, it's a mistake to conclude that the 1973 crisis alone sealed the business cycle's fate in the U.S. Nonetheless, the world learned rather quickly during that fateful year and beyond that rising oil prices are a factor that can create trouble for economies.

Economist James Hamilton observed in 2005 that "nine out of ten of the U.S. recessions since World War II were preceded by a spike up in oil prices."[11] A few years after the article was published, oil prices spiked to all-time highs in nominal terms—just as the Great Recession arrived. Coincidence? Perhaps, but Hamilton observed in another study, which analyzed the link between oil prices and the 2008-2009 recession:

> Whereas previous oil price shocks were primarily caused by physical disruptions of supply, the price run-up of 2007–08 was caused by strong demand confronting stagnating world production. Although the causes

---

[9] Yergin (1991), p. 606.
[10] Kissinger (1982), pp. 873-874.
[11] Hamilton (2005), p. 1.

were different, the consequences for the economy appear to have been similar to those observed in earlier episodes, with significant effects on consumption spending and purchases of domestic automobiles in particular. Absent those declines, it is unlikely that the period 2007Q4–2008Q3 would have been characterized as one of recession for the United States. This episode should thus be added to the list of U.S. recessions to which oil prices appear to have made a material contribution.[12]

Oil Prices and the Business Cycle: A Brief Review

The idea that sharp rises in oil prices will reliably cause or accompany a recession is patently false, as the historical record shows. But it's short-sighted to ignore the higher risk for the business cycle that follows dramatic price increases for a barrel of crude. It's impossible to say where exactly a price increase crosses the line and contributes to if not directly causes an economic downturn. Yet it's reasonable to assume that the higher prices go, the higher the potential for trouble.

Turning to the numbers proper, a rough rule of thumb that's implied by a simple review of history suggests that price hikes of 50% or more are likely to be connected with a new recession (Figure 9.1). But just to keep us guessing, it's clear that several 50%-plus increases have come and gone over the years without a slump. Take note too that the 1981-1982 recession arrived amid relatively stable oil prices, although that may be a byproduct of the short interval between the end of the previous recession and its successor.[13]

In any case, context matters. If oil prices are rising for the "right" reasons—strong economic growth, in particular—the risk of macro blowback from costly energy supplies may be relatively modest. But there are limits. At some point, rising energy costs takes a toll.

Exactly when there's a switch to a net negative, well, there are no hard red lines or infallible signals, in oil or any other indicator. As I've emphasized in previous chapters, every yardstick is flawed, a limitation that can be fatal in a statistical sense if one assumes that a lone data set will suffice. Working in a vacuum is never a good idea, and so it's essential to routinely monitor a broad range of key economic and financial data, including oil prices.

In search of deeper clarity, a number of economists have developed models for estimating the relationship between a given price increase and the potential for macro damage. For example, one study pointed to the surprise factor. The "oil price shock variable" is "likely to have a greater impact" on the economy "in an environment where oil prices have been stable, than in an environment where oil price movement has been frequent and erratic."[14] Hamilton (1996) observed that economic risk is substantially greater when higher oil prices overcome any price declines in the recent past. Another economist recently reminded that greater uncertainty about the

---

[12] Hamilton (2009), p. 215.

[13] One explanation for why oil prices didn't rise ahead of the 1981-1982 recession rests on the theory that the downturn was really an extension of the preceding contraction in 1980, which lasted a brief six months, according to the National Bureau of Economic Research. By this reasoning, the 1981-1982 recession was misdiagnosed as a separate event when in fact it was a continuation of the 1980 slide. If so, one can argue that that the U.S. endured a 1980-1982 downturn, which was triggered, in whole or in part, by the dramatic rise in oil prices in 1979.

[14] Lee, Ni, and Ratti (1995), p. 39.

macroeconomic horizon tends to create conditions that are ripe for trouble if there's an oil-related shock.[15]

No matter which model or narrative you favor, the details are subject to a fair amount of give and take when it comes to estimating a tipping point for the business cycle via oil. Maybe that's because tipping points vary, depending on the state of the economy, monetary policy, labor market conditions, and other factors that are in constant flux, as Blanchard and Gali (2009) reminded.

That's no excuse to ignore oil prices. It's clear that a substantial jump in the price of crude can have negative consequences for economic growth generally. Exactly when those consequences strike, or if they're large enough to contribute to a new recession, is forever unclear in advance. Nonetheless, history speaks convincingly when it comes to oil: it's foolish to ignore the commodity as a potential catalyst that, either alone or in concert with other trends, may push the economy over the edge.

Figure 9.1
Rolling 12-month % change in Spot Oil Price
(West Texas Intermediate), monthly

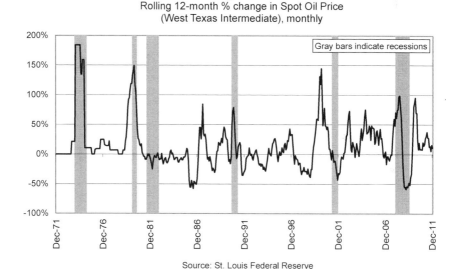

Source: St. Louis Federal Reserve

---

[15] Robays (2012).

Chapter 10

Follow the Money

Money supply

Money-supply targets fell out of favor at the Federal Reserve in the 1980s, but it's short-sighted to ignore the relationship between monetary aggregates and the business cycle. Indeed, the pro-cyclical connection between liquidity and economic fluctuations is one of the oldest empirical facts in the macro literature, dating to David Hume's 18th century observation that money and growth are intimately related.[1] As we'll see, the value of this link remains a fundamental tool for explaining the broad swings in economic activity.

Don't misunderstand: there's still plenty of debate about how to think about the nuances of this relationship. But the focus here is simply that monitoring the money supply is one of several key indicators for early clues about recession risk. History suggests this is a worthwhile effort. The persistence and power of money as a contributing factor in the economy's cyclical behavior is controversial only as a matter of degree. Economists have always argued over the extent of money's role on the real economy, and the discussion of what's relevant and what's not won't end anytime soon, if ever. But most analysts who study broad macro trends agree in principle that the monetary trend is a crucial variable for business cycle analysis.

Hume recognized money's integral role in economic fluctuations more than two centuries ago and his observation is no less relevant today. The historical record speaks loud and clear. Every recession since the late-1960s, for example, has been accompanied by a decline in the real (inflation-adjusted) monetary base (M0), as Figure 10.1 shows.[2] (The end date in Figure 10.1 has been truncated for clarity. The extraordinary monetary policy that began in late-2008 generated sharply larger swings in M0 compared with the historical record in the previous decades. With that in mind, Figure 10.2 tracks money supply changes from December 2006 onward for a clearer review of the trend.)

A key lesson from studying monetary history is that the annual change in the real level of M0 is closely connected with economic activity, just as Hume observed long ago. Economists in modern history continue to reaffirm Hume's central conclusion. Quite a few studies through the decades show that so-called monetary disturbances are closely linked with changes in economic output. A 2002 inquiry, for instance, found that "monetary shocks... significantly contribute to output and inflation cycles in all G-7 countries."[3] There's a debate in the academic community on whether monetary aggregates lead economic activity or vice versa. Some of the narratives

---

[1] Hume's 1752 essay "On Money" is one of the earliest examples in the economics literature of recognizing a positive correlation between changes in economic activity and the quantity of money in circulation.

[2] The U.S. monetary base, according to the Federal Reserve, is defined as the sum of currency in circulation and reserve balances (deposits held by banks and other depository institutions in their accounts at the Federal Reserve).

[3] Canova and De Nicolo (2002), p. 1131.

outlined in the literature suggest that a portion of the variety in the research results may be a function of different definitions of money.[4] But causality isn't all that important for the agenda at hand. The fact that real M0, in year-over-year terms, has a long history of going negative shortly before or during the early stages of recessions strongly suggests that this indicator is worth close attention for analyzing the business cycle.

Figure 10.1
Rolling 12-month % change in Real Monetary Base
St. Louis Fed Adjusted Monetary Base (monthly, seasonally adjusted)

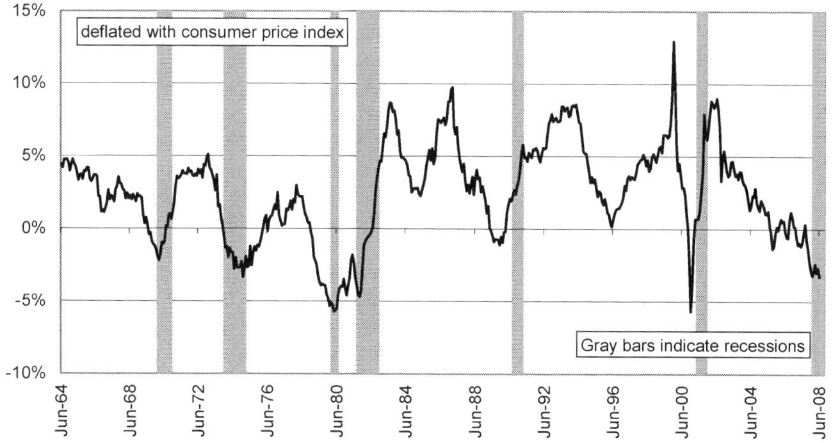

Source: St. Louis Federal Reserve

Many economists generally agree with this line of thinking, which can be summed up was follows: central banks have the power to minimize the severity of recessions through monetary policy. That power, should a central bank choose to deploy it, suggests that ill-timed or ill-conceived policy choices can exacerbate if not cause a negative turn in the business cycle. No wonder, then, that monetary policy has been widely criticized as it relates to the Great Recession of 2008-2009. Some analysts say the Fed and other central banks didn't react fast enough in response to the mounting macro troubles as 2008 unfolded. Robert Hetzel, for one, charged that in the spring of 2008,

> central banks became increasingly concerned that persistent headline inflation in excess of core inflation would destabilise expected inflation and compromise their inflation objectives. They then departed from lean-against-the-wind procedures by not lowering the funds rate in response to sustained decreases in rates of resource utilisation. The mild recession began to worsen in quarter three of 2008, while the appearance of world recession in autumn 2008 precipitated an enormous fall in wealth. Central banks remained slow to respond. As evidenced by the intensification of

---

[4] For example, see Sustek (2010).

recession in summer 2008, central banks caused declines in the real interest rate to lag behind declines in the natural interest rate.[5]

A similar charge was levied by Scott Sumner, a professor of economics at Bentley University who specializes in monetary affairs. "Monetary-policy officials simply failed to see the problem coming and did not react nearly quickly enough," he wrote in 2009.[6]

Figure 10.2
Rolling 12-month % change in Real Monetary Base
St. Louis Fed Adjusted Monetary Base (monthly, seasonally adjusted)

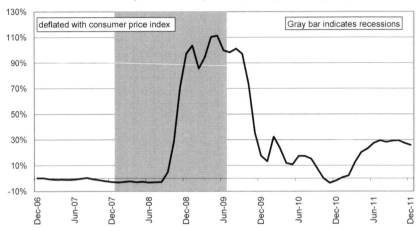

Source: St. Louis Federal Reserve

A History Of Error

The slow reaction to the onset of the Great Recession wasn't the first time that the central bank was criticized for lax monetary policy at a crucial point in the business cycle. A similar indictment has long been hurled at the Fed for its mistakes in the early 1930s. Indeed, a long line of research points to mismanagement during that period. As economist David Wheelock noted, economic conditions in 1931 and early 1932 were deteriorating while "monetary conditions were exceptionally restrictive."[7]

A key reason for the tight monetary policy in the face of economic contraction was the adherence to a form of the gold standard, which was still a controlling influence in the early thirties. The macro pressures of the Depression would eventually break the connection between the metal and monetary decisions, but in the early years of the decade the Fed's capacity to offset deflation was limited. As economist Barry Eichengreen thoroughly documented in *Golden Fetters: The Gold*

---

[5] Hetzel (2009), p. 21.
[6] Sumner (2011), p. 80.
[7] Wheelock (1997), p. 7.

Standard and the Great Depression, 1919-1939, the gold standard "magnified" the economic shock. Tying monetary policy to gold "was the binding constraint preventing policymakers from averting the failure of banks and containing the spread of financial panic" and it was a "central factor in the worldwide Depression." Not surprisingly, "recovery proved possible... only after abandoning the gold standard."[8]

The primary source for blaming the Fed for the macro debacle of the thirties is Milton Friedman and Anna Schwartz's monumental *A Monetary History of the United States*. Indeed, the modern era of monetary analysis begins with this research. Originally published in 1963, the tome has remained a staple in the literature, at least for those persuaded that monetary policy, for good or ill, is a key factor for the business cycle. Although this hefty volume takes a broad view of monetary policy across the century of economic history through 1960, it was one chapter in particular—"The Great Contraction, 1929-33"—that attracted attention and reordered opinion on the subject of cause and consequence.

At the time of the book's release, the dominant view was that a failure of capitalism and free markets triggered the Great Depression. Friedman and Schwartz changed the consensus, or at least offered a viable alternative for explaining the macroeconomic narrative. "The monetary collapse [of the early 1930s] was not the inescapable consequence of other forces, but rather a large independent factor which exerted a powerful influence on the course of events," Friedman and Schwartz wrote. Lest anyone misunderstand, they advised:

> The failure of the Federal Reserve System to prevent the collapse reflected not the impotence of monetary policy but rather the particular policies followed by the monetary authorities and, in smaller degree, the particular monetary arrangements in existence.
> The contraction is in fact a tragic testimonial to the importance of monetary forces.[9]

In time, the influence of Friedman and Schwartz's research resonated in the upper echelons of monetary authority and power. Perhaps the peak was 2004, when Ben Bernanke, a Fed governor at the time, explained that *A Monetary History of the United States* "transformed the debate about the Great Depression."[10]

Bernanke, of course, went on to become chairman of the Federal Reserve in 2006, a job that positioned him a few years later to pilot the central bank through the worst financial and economic crisis since the Great Depression. His stewardship at such a moment is ironic (or tragic, depending on your view of Bernanke's legacy) when you consider that this Princeton professor is a scholar of the Great Depression in his own right. "To understand the Great Depression is the Holy Grail of macroeconomics," Bernanke wrote in 1995.[11]

---

[8] Eichengreen (1992), p. xi.
[9] Friedman and Schwartz, [1963] 1993, p. 300.
[10] "Remarks by Governor Ben S. Bernanke. At the H. Parker Willis Lecture in Economic Policy, Washington and Lee University, Lexington, Virginia, March 2, 2004. 'Money, Gold, and the Great Depression'":
www.federalreserve.gov/boarddocs/speeches/2004/200403022/default.htm
[11] Bernanke (1995), p. 1.

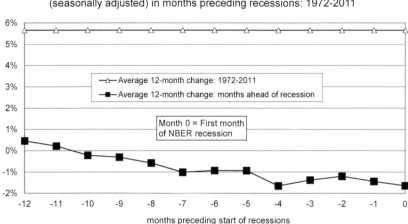

Figure 10.3
Average trailing 1-year % price change for real monetary base
(seasonally adjusted) in months preceding recessions: 1972-2011

Sources: St. Louis Federal Reserve, NBER, James Picerno

Whatever else we can say about the study of the Great Depression, particularly as it relates to monetary policy, it's inevitably a line of analysis that owes no small debt to Friedman and Schwartz. If there was any doubt about the extent of this debt, and how deeply *Monetary History* had penetrated into the halls of central banking policy, Bernanke set the record straight at a celebration of Friedman's 90th birthday. "I would like to say to Milton and Anna: Regarding the Great Depression. You're right, we did it. We're very sorry. But thanks to you, we won't do it again," Fed Governor Bernanke promised.[12]

Actually, Bernanke broke his promise, or so say some of his critics, such as Scott Sumner, as noted above. But for our purposes here, the key issue is whether monitoring monetary aggregates is worthwhile for analyzing recession risk in real time? The answer is clearly "yes," although it's essential to define money supply in a relevant manner in the context of identifying key turning points in the economy.

Base Information
The obvious challenge is choosing from the various benchmarks. Following in the footsteps of Friedman and Schwartz, we start with the monetary base—M0—as the standard factor linked with the to and fro of the business cycle. M0 is a relatively narrow definition of the money supply, which is its main appeal. M0 here is a reference to the most liquid slice of money, including cash in circulation. The central bank has direct influence over M0, as opposed to broader measures of money, such

---

[12] "Remarks by Governor Ben S. Bernanke. At the Conference to Honor Milton Friedman, University of Chicago, Chicago, Illinois, November 8, 2002. 'On Milton Friedman's Ninetieth Birthday'":
www.federalreserve.gov/boarddocs/speeches/2002/20021108/default.htm

as M1 or M2, which are also subject to decisions in the private sector and the Fed. M2, for instance, includes a variety of components, such as savings deposits and money market mutual funds.

According to Friedman and Schwartz, a positive co-movement exists between money supply and real economic activity over the course of the business cycle. Although there's an ongoing debate about the details of the link between money and real economic activity,[13] we can to some degree dispense with the particulars if the empirical record looks encouraging. As it turns out, that's what we find in terms of the real monetary base, as Figures 10.1 and 10.2 suggest.[14]

We can also see the trend across recent history in Figure 10.3, which summarizes the average annual change for real M0 in the months leading up to the start of recessions since 1972. It's clear that there's a tendency for the inflation-adjusted monetary base to contract on a year-over-year basis as the economy enters a downturn.

No, we can't count on this indicator to always provide an early warning of approaching contractions. No one variable is that reliable, in part because recessions aren't always triggered by the same set of events. For a time during the second half of 2005, for instance, the annual change in real M0 slipped into negative territory without a commensurate recession. But across the span of decades, false signals are the exception. A negative annual comparison is usually linked with the arrival of economic contraction in due course.

It may be different in the years ahead, thanks to the extraordinary and ongoing monetary policy choices in the wake of the Great Recession. But no one can be sure and so it's still reasonable to use M0 as one of several indicators for monitoring recession risk.

---

[13] As a starting point for exploring this debate, see Tobin (1970) and Freeman and Huffman (1991) for challenges to the views of macro-monetary relations a la Friedman and Schwartz (1963).

[14] M0 is defined here and throughout by the St. Louis Adjusted Monetary Base (AMBSL), available at: research.stlouisfed.org/fred2/series/AMBSL), and deflated with the Consumer Price Index (CPIAUCSL), which can be found at: research.stlouisfed.org/fred2/series/CPIAUCSL

Chapter 11

The American Dream and the Business Cycle

The housing market

Most economists will tell you that if you want to understand the business cycle, it's essential to look to the housing sector. Some dismal scientists even say it's *the* critical factor for the economy's ebb and flow. One professor states that "Housing *Is* The Cycle." Ed Leamer, writing in 2007, advised that "for long-run growth, residential investment is pretty inconsequential, but for the wiggles we call recessions and recoveries, residential investment is very, very important."[1] The reasoning, he concluded, is that "residential investment consistently and substantially contributes to weakness before the recessions...."[2]

Does that relationship warrant the claim that housing *is* the cycle? That may be going too far, but there's no doubt that the wide array of economic activity tied to housing casts a long shadow.

Leamer is far from alone in recognizing the power of residential real estate as a macroeconomic variable of consequence. A recent study of the 37 years through 2012 found a strong relationship between housing-market wealth and household consumption. In particular, rising home values are linked with higher consumption, and vice versa. "We do find strong evidence that variations in housing market wealth have important effects upon consumption," a trio of economists reported. In fact, the influence from the housing market on consumption is substantially greater compared with the wealth effect tied to the stock market, they found.[3] For example, they report:

> The decline in housing wealth from 2005-2009 was roughly thirty percent (somewhat more in real terms). Estimates of the elasticity of consumer spending range from 0.03 to 0.18, but those that are estimated with separate coefficients for up markets and down markets are consistently about 0.10 in down markets. That figure [0.10] implies that a decline of thirty-five percent in housing wealth would lower consumer spending by 3.5 percent. Consumption is about $10 trillion, and that, in turn, implies a decline in consumption of about $350 billion annually. To put those figures into context, consider the effects of the decline in housing production from 2.3 million units to 600 thousand, at $150,000 each. This implies reduced spending on residential capital of about $255 billion. Either has a large impact on the economy; together they have a very large impact.[4]

Another recent study reviewed a longer span (1920 through 2010) in search of insight on housing and the business cycle and discovered that "eleven of the most recent fourteen economic downturns in the U.S.—from the Great Depression that

---

[1] Leamer (2007), p. 10.
[2] Ibid., p. 13.
[3] Case, et al. (2012), p. 31.
[4] Ibid., p. 31.

began in 1929 to the Great Recession starting in late 2007—were led by declines in expenditure on new single-family and multi-family housing units."[5]

Another study in recent history that's worth considering on the subject of housing and the business cycle comes from a Federal Reserve paper that considers the "stall speed" concept (i.e., slow growth) as a tool for predicting recessions. One of the tests showed that "an observed annualized quarterly output growth rate of less than one percent [in gross domestic income[6]] could serve as a moderately useful warning sign that the economy is in danger of falling into recession."[7] The author noted that adding housing starts and Treasury yield curve data to the stall speed model improves the reliability of the forecasting signals.[8]

It's not hard to understand why. As economist Richard Yamarone advised, "never underestimate the economic importance of housing." The reasoning boils down to spending. An expanding housing market can promote economic growth, but a contracting market "can drag the overall economy into a deep recession."[9]

In the decade before the start of the Great Recession in January 2008, residential investment (which includes the construction of homes) amounted to 5.4% of U.S. gross domestic product, according to the Bureau of Economic Analysis. Housing's contribution to economic output, of course, fell sharply after the real estate crash that began circa 2006. From that peak to the fourth quarter of 2011, residential investment's share of GDP slumped by more than half, to 2.5%.[10]

It's unclear how quickly housing-related investment will rebound to historical levels, if ever, in the years ahead. Keep in mind, however, that the link between housing and the broader economy goes beyond construction and so this sector will remain a key factor for the business cycle, even if it's a diminished force relative to the past. Think about how much additional consumption takes place in connection with purchasing a home, particularly for first-time buyers. A new home initially is an empty home, which means that a fair amount of spending on furnishings is destiny soon after a new owner closes the deal. From furniture to appliances, every sale of a house implies some amount of additional spending in the near term future. If you consider rents paid to landlords and other services payments tied to housing, the sector's total economic activity as a share of GDP is considerably higher—14.9% in 2011's fourth quarter, for example.[11]

Housing By The Numbers
Let's turn to the data for a closer look at how the numbers compare with the arrival of recessions. Housing starts and housing permits, which are published monthly by

---

[5] Gjerstad and Smith (2010), pp. 1-2.

[6] Gross domestic income (GDI) measures economic activity as defined by the total income of the economy (wages, profits, etc.). In theory, GDI and gross domestic product (GDP) should be equivalent, although in both practice the two estimates of economic activity differ. Both GDI and GDP are calculated by the U.S. Bureau of Economic Analysis.

[7] Nalewaik (2011), p. 7.

[8] For a closer look at the relationship between the Treasury yield curve and the business cycle, see Chapter 4.

[9] Yamarone (2004), p. 159.

[10] Quoted in real (inflation-adjusted), seasonally adjusted annual rate terms.

[11] Ibid.

the U.S. Census Bureau, are widely followed as proxies of the sector's ebb and flow. The level of starts reflects the monthly pace of new residential construction, defined as single-family houses and multiple-family units (such as apartment buildings). The single-family units make up the majority of starts, routinely accounting for over one-half of residential construction activity. For the decade through the end of 2012, for example, single-family starts averaged 77% of the total.[12]

Figure 11.1
Rolling 12-month % change in housing starts and new private housing units authorized by building permits

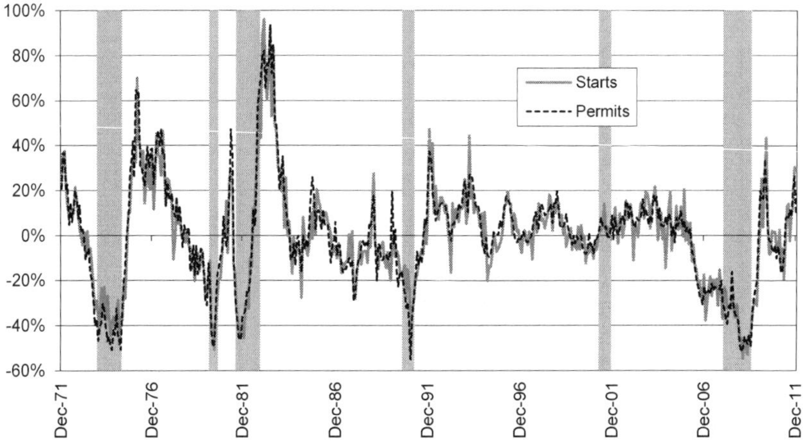

Source: St. Louis Federal Reserve

The counterpart starts is the monthly tally of newly issued housing permits. This data reflects the authorizations from local governments across the country that give homebuilders the green light to begin new construction on residential projects. In contrast with starts, which track actual groundbreaking activity, permits reflect plans for the future.

On a month-to-month basis, both series can be volatile at times and so it may be difficult if not impossible to see the trend in the short run. Reviewing the data on a year-over-year basis offers a clearer view (Figure 11.1). Comparing the annual percentage changes for starts and permits also highlights the fact that the two series track one another closely: the annual percentage changes post a high 0.95 correlation for the 40 years through 2011.

Given this relationship, it's no surprise that it's hard to distinguish starts from permits when plotting one-year percentage changes through time. As a result, starts and permits can be considered equivalent for monitoring the broad trend in housing and looking for clues about the business cycle. For simplicity, let's focus on permits as a proxy for housing's cyclical fluctuations.

---

[12] Based on monthly, seasonally adjusted annualized data.

Although the signals generated by permits aren't likely to diverge much from starts, permits have a slight edge, at least in theory. Newly issued authorizations to begin construction are indications of intent. Starts, on the other hand, reflect new construction activity. As such, permits can be thought of as a forward-looking benchmark, whereas starts tell us what's already happened in homebuilding. Yes, history reminds that this tends to be a subtle distinction based on the historical data and so we shouldn't over-emphasize the potential advantage or disadvantage in one or the other. Nonetheless, the Conference Board uses permits as one of the components in its leading indicator index.

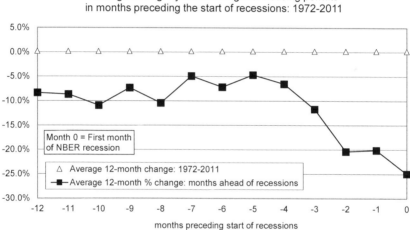

Figure 11.2
Average trailing 1-year % change for housing permits
in months preceding the start of recessions: 1972-2011

The bottom line: builders' plans for construction is a valuable proxy for tracking the housing market generally. "Keep a close eye on building permits because they lead housing starts by roughly one to three months," according to economist Bernard Baumohl.[13]

More importantly for our purposes, permits also provide some insight into the economic trend. Recessions tend to be associated with year-over-year declines in permits (and starts). It's true that these housing yardsticks can fall relative to year-earlier levels for reasons that aren't fatal for the business cycle and so we should be suspicious of using these indicators in isolation. That's true for every other data set, and so there's nothing particularly unusual here in recognizing that permits have shown a capacity for generating false warnings when it comes to looking for signs of recession risk.

But as discussed above, there are fundamental reasons for why we can't ignore housing. When permits are sliding on an annual basis, that's a dark sign. Reviewing

---

[13] Baumohl (2008), p. 181.

the seven recessions since the 1973-1974 episode shows that permits tend to be weak in the months ahead of a downturn. Why? Home builders are highly sensitive to ill winds blowing in the economy. Indeed, the annual change for permits tends to go sharply negative just ahead of a downturn's NBER start date (Figure 11.2), based on the historical record since the early 1970s.

Are permit declines alone sufficient to declare that the economy has reached a high state of recession risk? No. That higher standard still requires looking at the numbers in context with a broad set of indicators. But history shows that permits trending lower vs. year-earlier levels is a warning sign that shouldn't be dismissed. Looking back at the record since 1970 reminds that there's never been a recession without negative annual comparisons in permits. It may be different the next time, but to make that case you'd need to see convincing strength in several other indicators to offset a weak construction market.

PART III

NOWCASTING

Chapter 12

Nowcasting Recession Risk

A real-time roadmap for profiling the business cycle

In the previous chapters we've reviewed a spectrum of economic and financial indicators, each with varying degrees of value for assessing the current state of the business cycle. Now it's time to aggregate the data and study the business cycle from a top-down perspective using the numbers we've assembled.

A recurring theme in this book has been the simple reality that any one indicator, when used in isolation, can deceive us. Every recession is unique in some degree, which means that evaluating the economy is always a work in progress and so each indicator offers a shifting degree of insight. Although absolute confidence is an impossible standard, we can be reasonably sure that a carefully selected set of indicators will capture the essential information for estimating the general trend. If we had perfect knowledge of how the economy works, we'd know the exact list of factors that are crucial for our task. In that case, we could focus on the relevant yardsticks at each point in time and ignore the rest. But no one knows, in advance, which indicators will drive the next recession (or which ones will be worthless). And just to keep things interesting, the list of what's relevant is apt to change through time. That leaves us with the next-best option, which can be summarized as: 1) select a wide array of indicators that collectively represent the major influences on the economy through history; and 2) combine the signals to estimate and analyze the business cycle in real time.

Given our limited knowledge about the economy (especially when it comes to the economy's *future* performance), the main goal is less about predicting what's going to happen vs. reducing the doubt about the current state of macro conditions. This seemingly minor bit of intelligence can provide significant value for estimating the current and near-term threat of a new recession.

Our work begins by recognizing that the short list of decisive factors that create and accompany recessions is in constant flux. Let's emphasize once more that no one knows which combination of variables will determine the next downturn. As the previous chapters demonstrate, however, we have a reasonably good idea of where to find the likely suspects, even if some of them turn out to be weak or irrelevant down the road.

On that note, aggregating the data helps us to look past the noise of any one data set and focus on a comparatively robust approximation of the broad trend. Developing this strategic information begins by sensibly choosing a representative and diversified sample of metrics. Even if we could identify the optimal sample (we can't, of course), our job would only be halfway complete because we'd still need to decide on how to weight each of the factors according to their relative role in triggering the next recession. Here, too, we can only make informed guesses. There are several ways to estimate the optimal weights[1], although we're going to avoid this aspect of modeling entirely and instead favor a reasonable compromise when uncertainty is high: an equal-weighted mix.

The result is destined to be a crude measure of the economy's fluctuations, of course. But rough approximations in this context can still work fairly well, as the results from a real-time application suggest.[2] Nonetheless, we should be aware that our analysis at any point in time is merely one guesstimate in a continuum. Indeed, our estimates of the cycle will be constantly changing, in part because we're forced to work with data sets that suffer a variety of limitations.[3]

Our efforts to quantify the economy's fluctuations, in other words, will never rise beyond informed guesses. That's a hard limitation that endures. But depending on how we collect, manage and analyze the data, we can still learn a lot about the shifting nature of recession risk.

Assembling The Numbers

Since we're unsure of which corners of the economy and the financial markets will offer the most insight about the business cycle at each point in time, a workable compromise is building an equally weighted benchmark that incorporates inputs from a broad cross section of the macro landscape. How should we define "diversified" in this context? Let's show rather than tell by summarizing the indicators profiled in the previous chapters (Table 12.a).

There are, of course, many possibilities for building a short list of indicators. With tens of thousands of data series at the ready, the choices are virtually limitless. All the more reason to lay out a few ground rules. The main goal here is selecting data sets that collectively approximate a broad measure of economic activity. It's never really clear which indicators will offer the most value in the future in this task and so a naive equal-weighted mix is a practical solution if we don't have a convincing model to tell us otherwise.[4]

---

[1] One possibility is running a regression analysis on the changes for a given set of economic and financial indicators relative to the start dates of recessions through history. The resulting r-squared data for the observed values can provide intuition for quantifying how much each observation influences the outcome, i.e., the start of a new recession.

[2] For examples, search for the monthly economic updates at CapitalSpectator.com using the search phrase "US Economic Profile".

[3] Economic numbers are subject to revisions and are published with substantial time lags. Financial data are dispensed in real time and are immune to revisions, but these numbers are subject to short-term speculative distortions that don't always reflect the economic trend.

[4] Equal weighting makes sense generally if there's a high degree of uncertainty about the parameters for designing an optimally weighted model—a caveat that certainly applies to business cycle analysis. On paper, it's easy to use historical data to build an optimally weighted mix that worked well in the past. In practice, however, uncertainty is likely to give an edge to an equally weighted model that effectively hedges the risk of error when choosing indicators and deciding how to weight them in a model. The rationale for expecting that an equal-weight model will deliver sensible results is that this strategy makes no assumptions about parameters and so the hazards are low to non-existent for generating misleading results due to overfitting the model. (For an introduction to overfitting and a bibliography with related research, see Clark (2004)). For equal weighting's value in forecasting, see Dawes (1979).

It's also preferable to use indicators that are available on a timely basis. If our goal is identifying major downturns as early as possible, it's necessary to focus on numbers that are published frequently, with minimal time lags. That means that most of our attention turns to weekly (if available) and monthly numbers. For this reason, the quarterly GDP reports that receive so much attention in the press are of no use here since the data is published infrequently and arrives well after the fact.

Let's also ignore most of the so-called lagging indicators, particularly those with a history of reacting slowly to peaks in cyclical activity. For instance, consider business loans[5], which track the banking industry's willingness to lend and the corporate sector's appetite for credit. Although it's easy to assume that this data can help us identify cyclical peaks, the warning signs via business loans typically arrive too late in our search for timely insight for estimating the start of recessions.[6]

The track record for most, if not all, indicators is mixed, albeit in varying degrees. But beggars can still be choosy in a world of imperfect economic data by selecting indicators with comparatively lesser grades of deficiency. The good news is that we still have a wide array of possibilities. Too many, in fact.

Table 12.a						
	Market	Economic	Leading	Coincident	Survey	Real*
Markets						
Stock Market	•		•			
Treasury Yield Curve	•		•			
Credit Spread	•		•			
Oil Price	•		•			
Labor						
Private non-farm payrolls		•		•		•
Weekly hours worked		•		•		•
Employed-to-unemployed ratio		•		•		•
Iniital jobless claims		•	•			•
Consumer Spending						
Real personal consumption		•		•		
Real personal income		•		•		
Real retail sales		•		•		
Consumer sentiment index				•	•	
Business Activity						
Industrial production		•		•		•
Real mfg. & trade sales		•		•		
ISM mfg. index		•	•		•	
ISM non-mfg. index		•	•		•	
Macro Liquidity						
Monetary base			•			
Housing						
Residential bldg. permits		•	•			

* Real in the sense that the data focuses on economic activity that's not subject to price adjustments.

---

[5] Commercial and industrial loans, as defined by the seasonally adjusted weekly (TOTCI) and monthly (BUSLOANS) data sets at research.stlouisfed.org.

[6] Perhaps this is because bankers are focused on extending credit to borrowers with relatively strong financial profiles, which tend to improve as economic growth rolls on. The problem is that credit profiles are usually at their strongest when the business cycle peaks. As such, lending data can be a deeply misleading measure for assessing economic risk.

That brings up another point: in the necessary cause of developing a manageable list of relevant and timely indicators we must be mindful to avoid redundancy. To cite an extreme example to make a point, it's preferable to monitor five data series, each reflecting a different slice of the economy, vs. 50 indicators that are basically telling us the same thing. If we overlook this guideline, we may inadvertently give more weight to one part of the economy, or minimize another—lapses that may needlessly contaminate the quality of the analysis.

Avoiding redundancy doesn't demand all or nothing, however. Shades of gray are practical in some cases. In Chapter 6, we considered four measures of the labor market, each with a subtle but important distinction relative to the other three. Although subjectivity plays a role here, in this instance the use of four indicators is warranted because of the crucial link between jobs and the business cycle. In turn, eliminating any one (or more) of the four labor indicators would overlook valuable information not contained in the other three. As such, the four employment indicators are averaged so that we're still left with one employment metric, thereby sticking to an equal-weighting strategy relative to the other metrics.

Why not diversify for all categories of indicators? Several reasons, although the primary explanation is that the labor market has more nuance than, say, measuring industrial output or housing permits. The greater complexity in defining and measuring "the labor market" suggests that an extra level of detail is productive.

In any case, broad diversification in the final list of indicators is essential. If we had advance knowledge about which data sets will dispatch early and reliable signs of macro trouble, we could focus on those numbers alone. But no one has access to such foresight. Even so-called leading indicators are less than perfect and prone to all the usual limitations. The only solution is to routinely monitor a spectrum of benchmarks that are likely to provide a comprehensive and representative view of the business cycle through time.

Invariably, there will be debates about what exactly defines a "diversified" data set. But if Table 12.a falls short of the ideal, it's not too far off the mark, at least not conspicuously so. Certainly the major slices of the economy are represented, as noted by the category labels in bold on the vertical axis on the left side of table: the financial and commodity markets, along with the labor market, consumer spending, the business sector (sales and output), monetary liquidity, plus housing. Another dimension for categorizing the indicators is listed across the horizontal axis at the top of Table 12.a. Here too there's a degree of diversification to avoid relying too heavily on leading vs. coincident indicators, for instance.

The resulting list isn't the final word on building a robust set of economic and financial data sets for measuring the business cycle, but it's a reasonable first approximation. Meantime, keep in mind that all of the series in Table 12.a are publicly available, at no charge.[7]

Data Details
With a broad mix of data at our disposal, the next question: How to process the numbers in search of context for estimating recession risk? There are a number of possibilities, but an obvious place to start is with year-over-year percentage changes.

---

[7] See Appendix for details.

Reviewing data through this prism is practical for most indicators because annual changes minimize the short-term noise that can infect, say, monthly or quarterly reviews while capturing the broad trend that equates with business cycle fluctuations.

Monthly data in particular can swing wildly (partly due to seasonal factors), leaving a high degree of uncertainty about the trend when focusing on recent data comparisons. By contrast, the year-over-year percentage changes are considerably smoother, offering a clearer profile of how an indicator's evolving.

Table 12.b				
Indicator	**Transformation**		**Indicator**	**Transformation**
1. Labor Market Index [1]	1 yr % change		7. Consumer Spending Index [7]	1 yr % change
1a. Private non-farm payrolls	*1 yr % change*		*7a. Real Retail Sales*	*1 yr % change*
1b. Initial Jobless Claims [2]	*1 yr % chg (inverted)*		*7b. Real Pers. Cons. Expend.*	*1 yr % change*
1c. Employ.-to-Unemploy. Ratio	*1 yr % change*		8. Corporate Bond Spread	1 yr % chg
1d. Index of Agg. Weekly Hours [3]	*1 yr % change*		9. Real Monetary Base (M0)	1 yr % change
2. ISM Non-Mfg. Index [4]	% +/- neutral: 50 [5]		10. University of Michigan Consumer Sentiment Index	1 yr % change
3. US Stock Market (S&P 500) [2]	1 yr % change		11. Industrial Production	1 yr % change
4. ISM Manufacturing Index	% +/- neutral: 50 [5]		12. New Residential Bldg. Permits	1 yr % change
5. Spot Oil (W. Tex. Intermed.) [2]	1 yr % chg (inverted)		13. Real Mfg. & Trade Sales [8]	1 yr % change
6. Treasury Yield Curve (10 yr Note less 3 mo T-bill) [2]	current monthly spread [6]		14. Real personal income ex current transfer receipts	1 yr % change

1. Average 1-year % changes of payrolls, jobless claims, employed-to-unemployed ratio, and weekly hours index.
2. Based on average monthly data.
3. Production and Nonsupervisory Employees: Total Private Industries.
4. Data series begins Jan. 2008.
5. A neutral reading is assumed to be 50. The transformation is calculated as the % deviation for each monthly reading relative to 50.
6. Monthly difference: 10yr less 3mo % rates--multiplied by 10.
7. Average of 1-year % changes for real personal consumption expenditures & real retail sales.
8. Manufacturing & wholesale sales via BEA. Note: retail sales excluded.

Note: The Labor Market Index is considered as 1 indicator, comprised of the four indicators in blue cells. The Consumer Spending Index is comprised of 2 indicators, noted in blue cells. If one or more of the indicators in blue cells is published, the indicator is temporarily considered as the respective parent index data for the month until additional data is published.

Annual comparisons still leave plenty of room for debate about the implications for each new release. But we can find additional clarity for evaluating recession risk by aggregating the year-over-year changes, an adjustment that further limits the statistical noise. Let's put this idea to the test and examine how the 14 indicators in Table 12.a stack up in context with the historical record on recessions. But first, let's take a quick review of the indicators in terms of their transformations (Table 12.b).

The year-over-year percentage change is the primary adjustment for the indicators. But some data sets require an alternative form of analysis in order to make full use of their signals. In particular: The ISM indices that track manufacturing and non-manufacturing (services) activity are presented as percentage deviations from the neutral 50 level on a monthly basis. The reasoning is that the ISM indices are designed as diffusion indices to reflect above- or below-trend values. As such, monthly evaluations relative to a neutral 50 level maximizes the signal information for these indicators.[8]

---

[8] For example, a value of 52 for the ISM Manufacturing Index in, say, January would be recorded as +4.0% for the month, calculated as (52-50)/50.

The Treasury yield curve is also assessed on a monthly basis in terms of its monthly spread value (multiplied by 10 for easier comparison with the other indicators).[9] This choice stems from the literature, as discussed in Chapter 4.

Note too that several indicators in Table 12.b are published with daily or weekly frequencies. For direct comparison and analysis, all data sets are adjusted to monthly averages, if applicable. In addition, recall that the labor market and consumer spending indicators are composites of multiple data sets.

Finally, the percentage-change signals are inverted for two indicators—oil prices and initial jobless claims—in order to adjust for their countercyclical relationships with the business cycle.

Estimating The Trend
Let's turn to the main event: analyzing all the indicators in aggregated form in search of insight for assessing recession risk. As one test, consider the median percentage change for the 14 indicators in Table 12.b since the late-1960s, based on plotting the rolling 3-month-average change to smooth the volatility. We'll call this measure the Economic Momentum Index (EMI), with the historical record shown in Figure 12.1. As you can see, EMI values tend to go negative just before or during the early stages of recessions. In contrast, positive values are associated with economic growth.

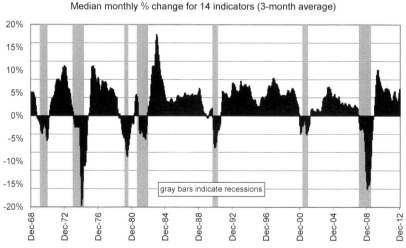

Figure 12.1
Economic Momentum Index (EMI)
Median monthly % change for 14 indicators (3-month average)

Sources: James Picerno, St. Louis Fed

---

[9] Assume a positive yield-curve spread of 200 basis points in December, for instance: the 10-year Treasury yields 5% and the 3-month T-Bill is 3%. In that case, the monthly value would be recorded as +20.0%, calculated as 5% less 3%, multiplied by 10, or (0.05-0.03)*10.

For another interpretation, consider the same 14 indicators after filtering the data via a diffusion index. This technique measures the percentage of indicators rising or falling, which is a simple but effective method for quantifying the overall bias in the data set. As Figure 12.2 illustrates, this diffusion index (Economic Trend Index, or ETI, as we'll label it) tends to mimic the information dispensed by the median change (EMI), albeit on a different scale. At or near the start of recessions, ETI falls below the 50% mark, which means that less than half of the 14 component indicators are trending positive.[10]

Figure 12.2
Economic Trend Index (ETI)
Monthly diffusion index for 14 indicators (3-month average)

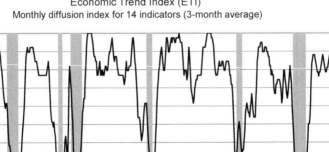

Sources: James Picerno, St. Louis Fed

Keep in mind that a diffusion index offers a slightly different perspective vs. the median change and so we should look for corroborating signals. The strongest warnings arise when the respective trends for ETI and EMI align in a clear manner. For example, in early 2008, ETI dropped below the neutral 50% mark and EMI slipped to negative values, dispensing two recession warnings at once.

We can also interpret the aggregated signals from the 14 indicators via a probit model, which transforms the index values into specific probabilities about recession risk.[11] As an example, the next chart transforms the ETI data into recession risk

---

[10] A 100% reading for ETI would indicate that all 14 indicators are trending positive; a 0% reading would reflect a state when no indicator is trending positive.

[11] A probit model is a form of regression analysis that estimates the probability of a given event, in this case the probability that a new recession has started. The details are relatively straightforward, as discussed in many econometric textbooks. You can also find guidance on the Internet (for example, see: en.wikipedia.org/wiki/Probit_model). For a more practical introduction, see the summary in "The Probability Model" in Estrella and Trubin (2006), p. 3, which outlines a simple probit model to interpret the Treasury yield curve for estimating recession risk.

probabilities. By comparing ETI with NBER recession periods through history, the probit model—a specialized form of regression analysis—estimates the likelihood of a new downturn. As Figure 12.3 shows, this methodology claims an encouraging track record, albeit one that comes with caveats. Specifically, the implied probabilities in Figure 12.3 use revised numbers and so the real-time estimates (i.e., before any revisions) dispensed a somewhat different perspective. Ideally, probability estimates should be computed frequently (several times a month). A regular schedule of estimating the probabilities will keep any revision-related surprises to a minimum.

Figure 12.3
Recession risk probabilities implied by the Economic Trend Index (ETI),
based on estimates using a probit model

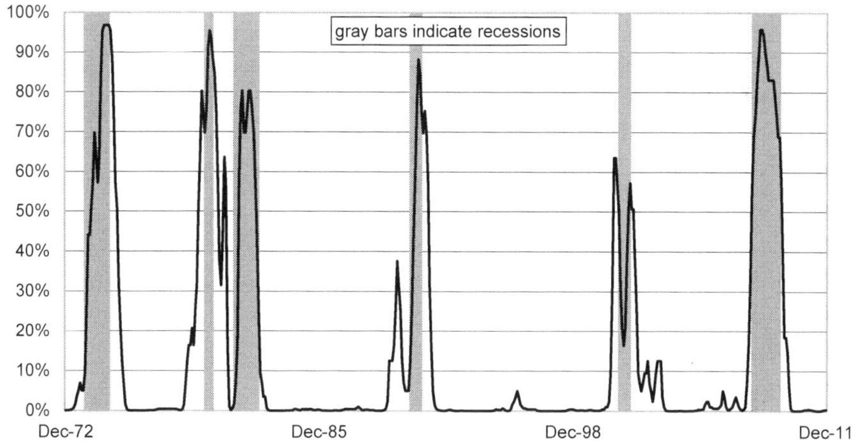

Source: James Picerno

Revision Risk
It's important to remember that revisions to initially reported data can be troublesome for real-time analysis. It's not usual for the first estimate of an economic indicator to change in subsequent updates, perhaps dramatically so. As a result, initial estimates of recession-risk probabilities may be misleading in terms of imparting reliable information about the business cycle. Even worse, revision-related volatility is apt to be high at major turning points in the business cycle.

The potential for spurious signals in the initial estimates of economic indicators has received attention in a number of studies over the years.[12] But one might wonder why are economic reports revised in the first place? The U.S. Bureau of Economic Analysis advised that it's less about correcting mistakes vs. satisfying the public's demand for information about the state of the economy. "It's not that the earlier estimate was wrong," the BEA recently explained. "Rather, it's the result of a delicate balancing act BEA performs to simultaneously achieve the two most

---

[12] Examples include Orphanides (2001) and Croushore and Evans (2003).

important qualities of its estimates—accuracy and timeliness. This government office, which calculates several key indicators for the U.S. economy, reasoned that

> The public wants accurate data and wants it as soon as possible. To meet that need, BEA publishes early estimates that are based on partial data. Even though these data aren't complete, they do provide an accurate general picture of economic activity. They capture the direction and trends of various components of the economy, providing valuable information that businesses and government leaders depend on and react to. They provide an "early read" on what's happening in the economy.[13]

We can reduce some of the potential for trouble by intelligently designing a business cycle index. There are at least three effective defenses for boosting the odds that the data that arrives in real time is a reasonably accurate approximation of the trend that will be revealed in the revised numbers in the weeks and months that follow. First, build an index with a broad, diversified set of indicators. Second, emphasize year-over-year changes. Third, include data from financial markets, which are immune to revisions.

As we've been discussing, ETI and EMI incorporate all three of these design features. Why should we expect that these techniques for building a business cycle index keep revision risk under control? The use of financial numbers is self-explanatory: What you see is what you get, now and forever. As for the economic numbers that may be revised (it's advisable to assume no less), the changes across a broad set of economic signals will, to some extent, cancel each other out.

Remember, revisions across time are a mix of positive and negative adjustments. Sometimes the updated data shows that a given change (up or down) for a particular indicator was higher or lower than initially estimated. For a mix of indicators, you'll often see positive and negative revisions through time, although negative revisions are more likely when recession risk is rising. Also, by focusing (mostly) on year-over-year changes, revisions to the latest data points will have comparatively lesser effects vs. looking at monthly or quarterly changes, which are prone to a higher degree of short-term noise. Indeed, data have usually gone through several rounds of revisions after 12 months. Looking at year-earlier numbers in real time probably tells us something that's close to the final read. As a result, revisions to the current numbers aren't likely to have a big impact for year-over-year comparisons.

Let's test this theory by comparing real-time vintage data with revisions for computing ETI and EMI. As Figures 12.4 and 12.5 show, the initial (vintage) and revised estimates of the indexes track one another closely if imperfectly in recent history, including before, during, and after the 2001 and 2008-2009 recessions.[14]

---

[13] blog.bea.gov/2012/07/23/revising-economic-indicators/

[14] Vintage data for a full sample of the indicators that comprise ETI and EMI are available as far back as the late-1990s. Complete vintage data sets become increasingly scarce for earlier starting dates and so the comparisons are limited to the last two recessions. Even then, the availability of vintage data is incomplete for some indicators—real manufacturing and wholesale trade sales, as published by the Bureau of Economic Analysis, are unavailable in vintage form, as far as I can tell. As a rough approximation, vintage data for this series is estimated by using a comparable data set in nominal terms from the Census Bureau (manufacturing and trade inventories and sales) and deflated using the Consumer Price Index.

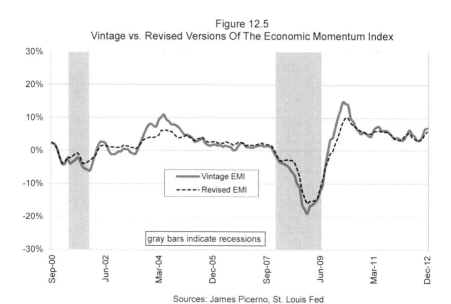

Figure 12.4
Vintage vs. Revised Versions Of The Economic Trend Index

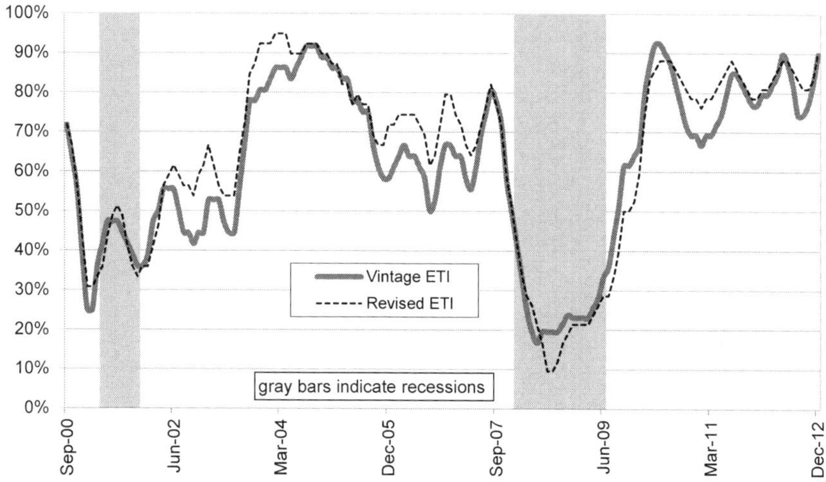

Sources: James Picerno, St. Louis Fed

Figure 12.5
Vintage vs. Revised Versions Of The Economic Momentum Index

Sources: James Picerno, St. Louis Fed

The main takeaway: the vintage versions of the benchmarks still provided valuable real-time signals about recession risk. Indeed, the initial signals generated by ETI and EMI were generally corroborated later on with the revised data. That's an encouraging sign, but there's no guarantee that vintage and revised data for ETI and EMI will continue to provide equivalent readings in real time for assessing business cycle risk. But history suggests that any differences will be short lived and minimal.

Nonetheless, regular updates of these indexes will boost the odds that misleading signals are the exception rather than the rule. As data is revised and the updates are incorporated into ETI and EMI values, the strategic value of the benchmarks will improve in the pursuit of reliable estimates of business cycle risk. Ideally, we should update ETI and EMI each and every time that one of the component series is updated, although monthly updates will probably suffice most of the time.[15] But when the economy is at or near a major turning point, frequent updates on a weekly basis are preferable in order to maximize the likelihood of acquiring accurate and timely signals.

Additional Context & Corroboration
With the details on building ETI and EMI behind us, let's focus on how to use these benchmarks in context with other data sets published elsewhere for some extra perspective.

Readers might wonder why we should trouble ourselves to calculate a proprietary index when comparable numbers are already available. Several reasons. First, crunching the data directly provides more timely insight vs. monthly indexes. In addition, building a proprietary index and updating it as new data is published enhances our familiarity with the various components and deepens the level of understanding of how the business cycle is evolving. If you're looking for a reasonably high degree of confidence about what the numbers imply for the economy, you need to get your hands dirty with the data. The deeper insight that flows from doing it yourself can be highly informative for deciding if the economy is genuinely deteriorating vs. enduring another round of temporary volatility that's unlikely to lead to a new recession.

In any case, context is important, no matter how deep your data dive, and so it's important to look for corroboration with any methodology. With that in mind, here's one way to proceed for using existing business cycle indicators to supplement the analysis via the signals dispensed by ETI and EMI. One benchmark that deserves monitoring is the Chicago Fed National Activity Index, which is updated towards the end of each month. The releases are "designed to gauge overall economic activity," according to the Chicago Fed's web site (chicagofed.org). The bank describes the index as "a weighted average of 85 existing monthly indicators" and positive (negative) values reflect economic activity that's above (below) trend; a zero value equates with the economy expanding at its historical trend rate of growth.[16] In particular, when the three-month moving average of the index (CFNAI-

---

[15] Updates of ETI and EMI, along with related analysis of the business cycle and financial markets, can be found at CapitalSpectator.com.
[16] The design of the Chicago Fed National Activity Index is based on a methodology outlined in Stock and Watson (1999).

MA3) falls below -0.70 after a period of growth, "there is an increasing likelihood that a recession has begun," as explained in each monthly press release for this benchmark.

The Chicago Fed index offers historical data from the mid-1960s on, although vintage numbers for this series start in January 2001. CFNAI-MA3's real-time signals for the 2001 and 2008-2009 recessions offered relatively early warnings, as Table 12.c shows. For the 2001 recession, the first publicly distributed release for CFNAI-MA3 indicated that a recession was underway in January of that year, which was revealed in real time on March 5. In subsequent months, the recession signal was maintained in the vintage releases.

For the Great Recession, the first real-time warning via CFNAI-MA3 arrived on March 24, 2008, when a press release indicated that an economic contraction commenced in February 2008.[17] Vintage data in subsequent monthly updates continued to reflect an ongoing contraction by way of index values that remained below the -0.70 mark.

Although the real-time record of CFNAI-MA3 provided relatively early signals of recession risk in 2001 and 2008, the question is whether one could have generated reliable signals a bit earlier? For example, based on vintage data for ETI and EMI, did these indexes offer an earlier real-time warning that a new recession had started relative to the vintage releases for CFNAI-MA3? Yes, as the vintage numbers for ETI and EMI show (Figures 12.4 and 12.5).

In the case of the 2001 recession, both ETI and EMI crossed their respective danger zones as 2001 began, based on vintage data. By the time the first CFNAI-MA3 recession signal was published (March 5, 2001), initial readings of ETI and EMI had been dispensing warnings of a broad economic contraction for several weeks.

A better test is analyzing the record for the 2008-2009 recession. CFNAI-MA3 was well established by this point, with several years of vintage numbers available for review. As shown, this index warned of recession with a public announcement on March 24, 2008. By contrast, the first vintage signal for ETI arrived in the January 2008 data point, which is the same start date for the recession as eventually announced by NBER. A slightly earlier warning sign was issued with EMI's vintage data in December 2007. The key question: Did

Table 12.c Chicago Fed Nat'l Activity Index Vintage 3-month averages		
Release Date	Index Date	Vintage Index Value
5-Mar-01	Jan-01	-0.71
3-Apr-01	Feb-01	-0.81
2-May-01	Mar-01	-0.80
31-May-01	Apr-01	-0.96
5-Jul-01	May-01	-1.04
2-Aug-01	Jun-01	-1.05
4-Sep-01	Jul-01	-0.82
20-Dec-07	Nov-07	-0.53
22-Jan-08	Dec-07	-0.67
25-Feb-08	Jan-08	-0.60
24-Mar-08	Feb-08	-0.87
21-Apr-08	Mar-08	-0.86
20-May-08	Apr-08	-1.24
23-Jun-08	May-08	-1.08
Source: Chicago Fed		

---

[17] NBER would eventually identify January 2008 as the first month of recession, nine months later, in a December 2008 press release.

these signals offered a real-time jump on CFNAI-MA3's March 24, 2008 warning? Yes, and here's why.

Most of the initially released data for ETI and EMI arrived with a lag of around one month. The financial numbers in the indexes are published in real time, of course, and are impervious to revisions, but the remaining economic series require several weeks to reach the public relative to the target month. For instance, retail sales figures for December are released by the Census Bureau midway in the following month. The main exception for data used in ETI and EMI: real manufacturing and trade sales, which the U.S. Bureau of Economic Analysis publishes roughly two months after the target month.[18] Even so, by the time this BEA series is published for the latest month, the other numbers for ETI and EMI for the month have been available for several weeks. As a result, by the time that the BEA numbers are revealed to the public, the release probably won't tell us something that wasn't already clear in the previously released indicators. In short, most of the data for ETI and EMI hits the streets a month or so after the fact. The January profile, for instance, is published in nearly complete form by the end of February.

Keep in mind that the opportunity to monitor the incoming data throughout each month allows us to see any deterioration building well before a complete set of monthly numbers is dispatched. That starts with real-time market components in ETI and EMI: stocks, oil prices, the Treasury yield curve, and the credit spread. In fact, by watching these markets separately, you can develop some intuition for how the "wisdom of the crowd" is pricing business-cycle risk. Although you shouldn't rely on markets alone for monitoring the economic trend, these financial indicators may dispense an early hint of economic trouble—in advance of reports on employment, industrial production, etc.[19]

The formal economic data arrives piecemeal, of course, but it's still worth monitoring on a weekly basis because the numbers provide incrementally deeper insight on the macro trend as each month progresses. The 2008-2009 recession offers an instructive example on how early insight for major turning points is usually a process of discovery across several weeks rather than a single "ah-ha" moment. Consider what was known in the early weeks of January 2008, at the start of the Great Recession, according to vintage data:

- Initial jobless claims in late-December 2007 and early January 2008 were rising on a year-over-year basis, a trend that had been in force for several months at that point.
- The annual rate of change in private payrolls in December 2007 slipped to the lowest increase in a year.
- Real retail sales turned negative on a year-over-year basis through December 2007 for the first time in five months, retreating the most in more than a year.
- The ISM Manufacturing Index slipped under the neutral 50 mark, dropping to its lowest level in nearly five years.

---

[18] In the interim, one can find a comparable and more timely data set to BEA's real manufacturing and trade sales figures via a report issued monthly by the Census Bureau: the Manufacturing and Trade Inventories Sales, which is published about six weeks after the end of the target month, or about two weeks ahead of BEA's update.

[19] The market-price components of ETI and EMI are analyzed at CapitalSpectator.com via the Macro-Markets Risk Index.

These numbers alone didn't provide overwhelming evidence that a new recession had started, but they certainly dropped some strong warnings of the potential for trouble. In the weeks to come, the number of econometric alarms mounted. If you were tracking the incoming numbers each week, it's likely that you'd have been increasingly skeptical of the economy's ability to steer clear of recession in the period leading up to CFNAI-MA3's March 24, 2008 release. By the time that the Chicago Fed report hit the streets, the telltale signs would have been compelling.

That's an important point about looking for credible signs that the business cycle is making a turn for the worse. Rarely if ever does the real-time time data profile change from sunny skies to convincingly dark clouds in one fell swoop. A gradual deterioration is the usual path, albeit with plenty of variation in the structure and pacing from one recession to the next. In any case, it's essential to maintain a degree of familiarity with the numbers in order to have some context for recognizing an authentic turning point in the broad trend.

Yes, there's always room for debate when it comes to real-time evaluation of the economy. Flawless signals are only available well after the fact. But just ahead of the Chicago Fed's March 24, 2008 release the numbers overall looked quite damning—an interpretation that was confirmed with the publication of CFNAI-MA3's recession signal.

The next time could be different, of course. The signals may arrive later, or dispense weaker warnings in the early stages of a developing recession. Much depends on the nature of the downturn. Is it the result of a financial crisis? Or something less ominous and therefore more subtle? No one really knows how future contractions will play out, of course. But as we've learned on the previous pages, recessions don't stay hidden for long... at least for those analysts who are looking in the right places and through a reliable econometric lens.

Looking Into The Future

For additional context, a bit of short-term forecasting can help squeeze more insight out of the data. Projecting economic indicators is risky, of course. But if we're careful and use a robust system to peer ahead by just a few months, the analysis can offer a valuable *supplement* to the nowcasting process outlined above. Indeed, if we regularly generate forecasts and track the fluctuations of predictions in context with the actual data that follows, the ebb and flow of the forward-looking estimates can improve our understanding of how the business cycle is changing.

For example, if the forecasts are routinely trending lower over a period of time, and the subsequently updated reports from the government and other sources generally confirm the descent, that's a stronger sign for deciding that the economic outlook is deteriorating. It's also a more timely warning vs. simply waiting for official reports to be published.

One approach that's proven helpful is using a forecasting technique known as an autoregressive integrated moving average (ARIMA) to generate an array of predictions that we can aggregate for a relatively dependable big-picture outlook. An ARIMA model is a type of regression analysis that combines trend analysis of the actual data with the forecast blunders in search of patterns for anticipating the future. As Kacapyr (1996) explained, "ARIMA models create forecasts based on the past values of the data series and the past forecast errors. By including moving-average terms in the analysis, we are attempting to improve forecast accuracy by taking into account previous forecast errors."[20]

As an example, consider the forecasts in Figure 12.6 vs. the actual data that was eventually reported.[21] The bars represent forecasts of the Economic Trend Index (ETI) at various times from mid-2013 through early 2014; the circles show the actual ETI data, based on a complete set of subsequently published indicators (as of March 2014). Note how the forecasts for each month change as new data becomes available. Observe too that the forecasts offer a reasonably close approximation of the actual data that followed. That's not unusual for at least two reasons:

- The projections target a broadly defined benchmark of economic activity (i.e., ETI), which is relatively stable compared with any one its component indicators.
- The projections are routinely combined with the actual data that's available at each forecasting period—a combination that helps to stabilize the reliability of the predictions relative to using only estimated numbers.

Although the forecast for any one of ETI's 14 indicators is likely to be wrong, the errors may cancel each other out to some degree by way of aggregating a spectrum of predictions. As a result, projections of ETI for the near term have been relatively reliable guesstimates of the full set of monthly numbers that were eventually published.[22]

How much confidence should we put in forecasts of the economy generally? Not much. Indeed, this book makes the case for focusing on the existing data as it's published as the first and best strategy for evaluating business cycle risk in real time—i.e., nowcasting. History shows this to be the superior methodology for analyzing the business cycle relative to predicting what may or may not happen down the road. But a bit of cautious predicting doesn't hurt... assuming we don't let this tail wag the dog or indulge in a dangerous game of forecasting in the extreme with shaky models or looking far into the future. But prudently applied as a tool for adding more context to the foundation of analyzing the real-time data as published, forecasting can be constructive.

One example is regularly generating forecasts and comparing them with the actual data. Ideally, the forecast errors will vary randomly. In times of rising economic stress, the actual data may routinely fall short of the forecasts—an additional warning signal. The key assumption for thinking that the forecasting model above will be helpful is the use of multiple indicators and forecasts. By design,

---

[20] Kacapyr (1996), p. 99.

[21] Figure 12.6 was originally published on Dec. 19, 2013 on CapitalSpectator.com and is reproduced here with the available data as of that date.

[22] Based on the track record for vintage and revised data for 2011-2013, as published in real time for the U.S. Economic Profile updates at the author's web site, CapitalSpectator.com. The ARIMA forecasts that are used in the projections are generated in the "forecast" package for R, a statistical software environment. Note that the forecasts are "optimized" according to the Akaike information criterion (AIC), which provides a quantitative measure of the quality of the ARIMA model's output, i.e., the goodness of fit. AIC-based analysis can assist in the goal of minimizing the forecast errors by identifying superior prediction techniques. For details, see Hyndman and Khandakar (2008).

the index (ETI) we're trying to anticipate is relatively steady across short-term horizons. That makes our job of peering ahead with ETI somewhat easier than predicting the near-term changes for, say, industrial production.

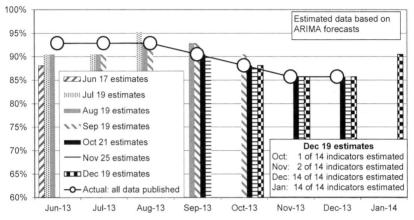

Figure 12.6   19 Dec 2013
Economic Trend Index: Actual vs. Projections
% of 14 key leading and coincident indicators trending positive for
economic growth (3-month average, plotted monthly)

Source: CapitalSpectator.com

You can take a short cut with an existing business cycle benchmark. But in search of a higher level of confidence, there's no substitute for doing it yourself. On that point, let's conclude where we began—with a quote from the statistician George E. P. Box:

> In applying mathematics to subjects such as physics or statistics we make tentative assumptions about the real world which we know are false but which we believe may be useful nonetheless. The physicist knows that particles have mass and yet certain results, approximating what really happens, may be derived from the assumption that they do not. Equally, the statistician knows, for example, that in nature there never was a normal distribution, there never was a straight line, yet with normal and linear assumptions, known to be false, he can often derive results which match, to a useful approximation, those found in the real world.[23]

---

[23] Box (1976), p. 792.

Appendix

Most of the economic and financial indicators cited and analyzed in this book are available gratis through the St. Louis Federal Reserve's FRED (Federal Reserve Economic Data) database: research.stlouisfed.org/fred2/

The main exception is the real manufacturing and trade sales data, which is published by the U.S. Bureau of Economic Analysis: bea.gov/national/index.htm in the National Economic Accounts database under the "Underlying Detail Tables" section. For vintage data, refer to the St. Louis Federal Reserve's ALFRED (ArchivaL Federal Reserve Economic Data) database: alfred.stlouisfed.org/

Additional web sites that offer data that's useful for business cycle analysis:

Federal Reserve Bank of Philadelphia
www.phil.frb.org/research-and-data/

Federal Reserve Bank of Chicago
www.chicagofed.org/webpages/research/data/index.cfm

To access the primary datasets cited in this book, the following tickers apply for the St. Louis Fed's FRED database:

Private non-farm payrolls (USPRIV)
Initial jobless claims (ICSA)
Employment-to-unemployment ratio (CE16OV/UNEMPLOY)
Index of weekly hours worked (AWHI)
US stock market/S&P 500 (SP500)
Real personal income ex-current transfer receipts (W875RX1)
ISM Manufacturing Index (NAPM)
Spot price for crude oil (OILPRICE and MCOILWTICO)
Real personal consumption expenditures (PCEC96)[1]
Real retail sales (RSALES and RRSFS)
Treasury yield curve (GS10 and TB3MS)
Corporate bond spread (BAA and AAA)[2]
Real monetary base (AMBSL/CPIAUCSL)
University of Michigan Consumer Sentiment Index (UMCSENT)[3]
Industrial production (INDPRO)
New residential building permits (PERMIT)
ISM Non-Manufacturing Index (NMFCI)
Real manufacturing and trade sales (see reference above)

---

[1] PCEC96 begins in 1999. For a longer time series, you can construct a deflated data set for use with year-over-year changes with the ratio: nominal personal consumption expenditures (PCE)/Personal Consumption Expenditures: Chain-type Price Index (PCEPI).

[2] For the high-yield bond yield spread, see: BofA Merrill Lynch US High Yield Master II Option-Adjusted Spread (BAMLH0A0HYM2).

[3] Published with a 6-month lag. For current data, see: press.sca.isr.umich.edu/ and www.bloomberg.com/quote/CONSSENT:IND

Bibliography

Achuthan, Lakshman and Anirvan Banerji, 2004. *Beating the Business Cycle: How to Predict and Profit From Turning Points In the Economy*, New York: Currency Doubleday.

Aldenhoff, Frank-Oliver, 2007. "Are economic forecasts of the International Monetary Fund politically biased?", *Review of International Organizations* 2: 239-260, Vol. 2, no. 3, pp. 239-260.

Ang, Andrew, Monika Piazzesi, and Min Wei, 2006. "What does the yield curve tell us about GDP growth?", *Journal of Econometrics*, Vol. 131, Nos. 1-2, pp. 359-403.

Atkeson, Andrew and Lee E. Ohanian, 2001. "Are Phillips Curves Useful for Forecasting Inflation?", *Federal Reserve Bank of Minneapolis Quarterly Review*, Vol. 25, no. 1, pp. 2–11.

Aruoba, S. Boragan, Francis X. Diebold, and Chiara Scotti, 2009. "Real-Time Measurement of Business Conditions," *Journal of Business and Economic Statistics*, Vol. 27, No. 4, pp. 417-427.

Backhouse, Roger E., 2010. *The Puzzle of Modern Economics: Science or Ideology?*, Cambridge: Cambridge University Press.

Backus, David K., Bryan R. Routledge Stanley E. Zin, 2010. "The cyclical component of U.S. asset returns," working paper.

Bachman, Daniel, 2010. "The Information Content of the ISM Purchasing Managers' Survey," working paper.

Baker, Dean, 2008. "The housing bubble and the financial crisis," *Real-World Economics Review* (Center for Economic and Policy Research), no. 46.

_____, 2010. "Blame It On The Bubble," www.guardian.co.uk, March 8.

Bates, J.M. and C.W.J. Granger, 1969. "The Combination of Forecasts," *Operations Research Quarterly*, Vol. 20, No. 4, pp. 451-468.

Baumohl, Bernard, 2008. *The Secrets of Economic Indicators: Hidden Clues to Future Economic Trends and Investment Opportunities*, Upper Saddle River, New Jersey: Pearson Prentice Hall.

Belke, Ansgar, Christian Dreger and Frauke de Haan, 2011. "Energy Consumption and Economic Growth: New Insights Into the Cointegration Relationship," *Energy Economics*, Vol. 33, No. 5, pp. 782-789.

Benston, Liz, 2009. "Sued by Fontainebleau, Banks Could Cite 'Act of God' As Defense for Refusing Funds," *Las Vegas Sun*, April 29.

Berge, Travis J. and Oscar Jorda, 2010. "Future Recession Risks," *Economic Letter* (Federal Reserve Bank of San Francisco), no. 2010-24.

_____, 2012. "Evaluating the Classification of Economic Activity into Recessions and Expansions," *American Economic Journal: Macroeconomics*, Vol. 3, no. 2, pp. 246–77.

Bernanke, Ben. S., 1995. "The Macroeconomics of the Great Depression: A Comparative Approach," *Journal of Money, Credit and Banking*, Vol. 27, No. 2, pp. 1-28.

Bernanke, Ben S. and Mark Gertler, 1995. "Inside the black box: The credit channel of monetary policy transmission," *Journal of Economic Perspectives*, Vol. 9, No. 4, pp. 27-48.

Bernanke, Ben S., Mark Gertler and Simon Gilchrist, 1999. "The financial accelerator in a quantitative business cycle framework," in *Handbook of Macroeconomics, Vol. 1C*, eds. John B. Taylor and Michael Woodford, Elsevier Science, North-Holland: Amsterdam, (Chapter 21) pp. 1341-1393.

Bernard, Henri, and Stefan Gerlach, 1996. "Does the term structure predict recessions? The international evidence," *International Journal of Finance & Economics*, Vol. 3, No. 3, pp. 195-278.

Besomi, Daniele, 2010. "'Periodic crises': Clement Juglar between theories of crises and theories of business cycles," in *A Research Annual (Research in the History of Economic Thought and Methodology, Vol. 28)*, eds. Jeff E. Biddle and Ross B. Emmett, Bingley, U.K.: Emerald Group Publishing, pp. 169-283.

Black, Henry Campbell, [1891] 1991. *A Dictionary of Law*, Clark, New Jersey: Lawbook Exchange.

Blanchard, Oliver J. and Jordi Gali, 2009. "The Macroeconomic Effects of Oil Price Shocks: Why Are the 2000s So Different From the 1970s?", in *International Dimensions of Monetary Policy*, eds. Jordi Gali and Mark Gertler, University of Chicago Press: Chicago, (Chapter 7), pp. 373-428.

Binder, Denis, 1996. "Act of God? or Act of Man?: A Reappraisal of the Act of God Defense in Tort Law," *The Review of Litigation*, Vol. 15, No. 1, pp. 1-79.

Box, George E. P., 1976. "Science and Statistics," *Journal of the American Statistical Association*, Vol. 71, No. 356, pp. 791-799.

Bram, Jason and Sydney Ludvigson, 1998. "Does Consumer Confidence Forecast Household Expenditure? A Sentiment Index Horse Race," *Economic Policy Review* (Federal Reserve Bank of New York), Vol. 4, No. 2, pp. 59–78.

Buiter, Willem, 2009. "The unfortunate uselessness of most 'state of the art' academic monetary economics," VoxEU.org (Centre for Economic Policy Research), March 6, 2009. Retrieved Mar. 19, 2012: www.voxeu.org/index.php?q=node/3210

Burns, Arthur F., 1946. "Economic Research and the Keynesian Thinking of Our Times," in *Twenty-Sixth Annual Report of the National Bureau of Economic Research*, New York: National Bureau of Economic Research, pp. 3-25.

_____, 1960. "Progress Towards Economic Stability," *American Economic Review*, Vol. 50, No. 1, pp. 1-19.

Burns, Arthur F. and Wesley C. Mitchell, 1946. *Measuring Business Cycles*, New York: National Bureau of Economic Research.

Cantillon, Richard, [1755] 2010. *An Essay on Economic Theory. An English translation of Richard Cantillon's Essai sur la Nature du Commerce en Général*, trans. Chantal Saucier, ed. Mark Thornton, Auburn, Alabama: Ludwig von Mises Institute.

Canova, Fabio and Gianni De Nicolo, 2002. "Monetary disturbances matter for business fluctuations in the G-7," *Journal of Monetary Economics*, Vol. 49, No. 6, pp. 1131–1159.

Carroll, Christopher D., Jeffrey C. Fuhrer, and David W. Wilcox, 1994. "Does Consumer Sentiment Forecast Household Spending? If So, Why?", *American Economic Review*, Vol. 84, No. 5, pp. 1397–1408.

Case, Karl E., John M. Quigley and Robert J. Shiller, 2012. "Wealth Effects Revisited 1975-2012," Cowles Foundation discussion paper No. 1884.

Chen, Nai-Fu, 1991. "Financial Investment Opportunities and the Macroeconomy," *Journal of Finance*, Vol. 46, No. 2, pp. 529-554.

Chauvet, Marcelle and James D. Hamilton, 2006. "Dating Business Cycle Turning Points," in *Nonlinear Time Series Analysis of Business Cycles (Contributions to Economic Analysis, Vol. 276)*, eds. Badi H. Baltagi and Efraim Sadka, Bingley, U.K.: Emerald Group Publishing, pp.1-54.

Chauvet, Marcelle and Jeremy Piger, 2008. "A Comparison of the Real-Time Performance of Business Cycle Dating Methods," *Journal of Business & Economic Statistics*, Vol. 26, No. 1, pp. 42–49.

Claessens, Stijn M., Ayhan Kose and Marco E. Terrones, 2008. "What Happens During Recessions, Crunches and Busts?", IMF working paper 08/274.

Clark, Todd E., 2004. "Can out-of-sample forecast comparisons help prevent overfitting?", *Journal of Forecasting*, Vol. 23, No. 2, pp. 115-139.

Clemen, Robert T., 1989. "Combining forecasts: A review and annotated bibliography", *International Journal of Forecasting*, Vol. 5, No. 4, pp. 559-583.

Cochrane, John, 2005. *Financial markets and the real economy*, Hanover, Mass: Now Publishers.

_____, 2009. "Lessons from the Financial Crisis," *Regulation* (Cato Institute), Winter 2009-2010, p. 34.

Congdon, Tim and Gordon Pepper, 2009. "How to stop the recession," *Daily Telegraph* (U.K.), January 7.

Congressional Budget Office, 2001. "CBO's Method for Estimating Potential Output: An Update," August.

Covas, Francisco and Wouter J. Den Haan, 2012. "The Role of Debt and Equity Finance Over the Business Cycle," *Economic Journal*, Vol. 122, No. 565, pp 1262–1286.

Covel, Michael W., 2009. *Trend Following: How Great Traders Make Millions in Up or Down Markets*, New York: FT Press.

Cornell, Bradford, 2010. "Economic Growth and Equity Investing," *Financial Analysts Journal*, Vol. 66, No. 1, pp. 54-64.

Cox, Garfield V., 1929. *An Appraisal of American Business Forecasts*, University of Chicago Press, Chicago.

Crone, Theodore M., 2006. "What a New Set of Indexes Tells Us About State and National Business Cycles," *Business Review* (Federal Reserve Bank of Philadelphia), First Quarter, pp. 11-24.

Croushore, Dean and Charles L. Evans, 2003. "Data revisions and the Identification of Monetary Policy Shocks," working paper No. 03-1 (Federal Reserve Bank of Philadelphia).

Dal-Pont Legrande, Muriel and Harald Hagemann, 2007. "Business Cycles in Juglar and Schumpeter," *History of Economic Thought* (Japan), Vol. 49, No. 1, pp. 1-18.

Davis, Steven J. and John Haltiwanger, 2001. "Sectoral job creation and destruction responses to oil price changes," *Journal of Monetary Economics*, Vol. 48, No. 3, pp. 465-512.

Dawes, Robyn M., 1979. "The robust beauty of improper linear models in decision making," *American Psychologist*, Vol. 34, No. 7, pp. 571-582.

Deane, Marjorie and Robert Pringle, 1995. *The Central Banks*, New York: Viking.

Diebold, Francis X. and Glenn D. Rudebusch, 1989. "Scoring the Leading Indicators," *Journal of Business,* Vol. 62, No. 3, pp. 369-391.

_____, 1991a. "Forecasting Output with the Composite Leading Index: A Real-Time Analysis," *Journal of the American Statistical Association*, Vol. 86, No. 415, pp. 603-610.

_____, 1991b. "Turning Point Prediction With the Composite Leading Index: An Ex Ante Analysis," in *Leading Economic Indicators: New Approaches and Forecasting Records*, eds. Kajal Lahiri and Geoffrey H. Moore, Cambridge: Cambridge University Press, 1991, pp. 231-256.

_____, 2001. "Five Questions about Business Cycles," *Economic Review* (Federal Reserve Bank of San Francisco), pp. 1-15.

Dornbusch, Rudiger, 1997. "How Real Is U.S. Prosperity?", in World Economic Laboratory Columns, Massachusetts Institute of Technology, December; cited in *Beyond Shocks: What Causes Business Cycles?*, eds. Jeffrey G. Fuhrer and Scott Schuh, Federal Reserve Bank of Boston Conference Series No. 42, 1998, p. 37.

Dreher, Axel, Silvia Marchesi, and James Raymond Vreeland, 2007. "The Politics of IMF Forecasts," CESifo working paper No. 2129.

Duarte, Agustin, Ioannis A. Venetis and Ivan Paya, 2005. "Predicting real growth and the probability of recession in the Euro area using the yield spread." *International Journal of Forecasting*, Vol. 21, No. 2, pp. 261-277.

Dueker, Michael, 2005. "Dynamic Forecasts of Qualitative Variables: A Qual VAR Model of U.S. Recessions," *Journal of Business & Economic Statistics*, Vol. 23, No. 1, pp. 96–104.

Dynan, Karen E. and Dean M. Maki, 2001. "Does Stock Market Wealth Matter for Consumption?", Finance and Economics Discussion Series, No. 2001-23 (Board of Governors of the Federal Reserve System).

Eichengreen, Barry J., 1992. *Golden Fetters: The Gold Standard and the Great Depression, 1919-1939*, New York: Oxford University Press.

Emmons, William R., 2012. "Don't Expect Consumer Spending To Be the Engine of Economic Growth It Once Was," *The Regional Economist* (Federal Reserve Bank of St. Louis), Vol. 20, No. 1, "Online extra" article: www.stlouisfed.org/publications/re/articles/?id=2201

Estrella, Arturo and Jeffrey C. Fuhrer, 2003. "Monetary Policy Shifts and the Stability of Monetary Policy Models," *Review of Economics and Statistics*, Vol. 85, No. 1, pp. 94-104.

Estrella, Arturo and Gikas A. Hardouvelis, 1991. *Journal of Finance*, "The Term Structure as a Predictor of Real Economic Activity," Vol. 46, No. 2, pp. 555-576.

Estrella, Arturo and Frederic S. Mishkin, 1996. "The Yield Curve as a Predictor of U.S. Recessions," *Federal Reserve Bank of New York Current Issues In Economics and Finance*, Vol. 2, No. 7, pp. 1-6.

_____, 1997. "The predictive power of the term structure of interest rates in Europe and the United States: Implications for the European Central Bank," *European Economic Review*, Vol. 41, No. 7, pp. 1375-1401.

_____, 1998. "Predicting U.S. Recessions: Financial Variables as Leading Indicators," *Review of Economics and Statistics*, Vol. 80, No. 1, pp. 45-61.

Estrella, Arturo and Mary R. Trubin, 2006. "The Yield Curve as a Leading Indicator: Some Practical Issues," *Federal Reserve Bank of New York Current Issues In Economics and Finance*, Vol. 12, No. 5, pp. 1-7.

Fama, Eugene F., 1990. "Stock Returns, Expected Returns, and Real Activity," *Journal of Finance*, Vol. 45, No. 4, pp. 1089-1108.

Faust, Jon, Simon Gilchrist, Jonathan H. Wright, and Egon Zakrajsek, 2011. "Credit Spreads as Predictors of Real-Time Economic Activity: A Bayesian Model-Averaging Approach," NBER working paper No. 16725.

Ferson, Wayne E. and Campbell R. Harvey, 1991. "The Variation of Economic Risk Premiums," *Journal of Political Economy*, Vol. 99, No. 2, pp. 385-414.

Fisher, Irving, 1925. "Our Unstable Dollar and the So-Called Business Cycle," *Journal of the American Statistical Association*, Vol. 20, No. 150, pp. 179-202.

_____, [1926] 1973. "I Discovered the Phillips Curve: 'A Statistical Relation between Unemployment and Price Changes'" *Journal of Political Economy*, Vol. 81, No. 2, Part 1, pp. 496-502, reprinted from *International Labour Review*, 1926.

_____, 1933. "The Debt-Deflation Theory of Great Depressions," *Econometrica*, Vol. 1, No. 4, pp. 337-357.

Frankel, Jeffrey, 2011. "Over-optimism in Forecasts by Official Budget Agencies and Its Implications," NBER working paper No. 17239.

Freedman, David H., 2010. *Wrong: Why experts keep failing us—and how to know when not to trust them*, Little, Brown: New York.

Freeman, Scott and Gregory W. Huffman, 1991. "Inside Money, Output, and Causality," *International Economic Review*, Vol. 32, No. 3, pp. 645-667.

Friedman, Milton, 1953. "The Methodology of Positive Economics," in *Essays In Positive Economics*, Chicago: University of Chicago Press, pp. 3-43.

_____, 1968. "The Role of Monetary Policy," *American Economic Review*, Vol. 58, No. 1, pp. 1-17.

Friedman, Milton and Anna Jacobson Schwartz, [1963] 1993. *A Monetary History of the United States, 1867-1960*, Princeton: Princeton University Press.

Frumkin, Norman, 2010. *Recession Prevention Handbook: Eleven Case Studies, 1948-2007*, Armonk, New York: M.E. Sharpe.

Fuhrer, Jeffrey C., 1988. "On The Information Content Of Consumer Survey Expectations," *Review of Economics and Statistics*, Vol. 70, No. 1, pp. 140–144.

Gardner, Dan, 2011. *Why Expert Predictions Are Next to Worthless, and You Can Do Better*, Dutton: New York.

Gali, Jordi and Luca Gambetti, 2009. "On the Sources of the Great Moderation," *American Economic Journal: Macroeconomics*, Vol. 1, No. 1, pp. 26-57.

Gilchrist, Simon, Vladimir Yankov and Egon Zakrajsek, 2009. "Credit Market Shocks and Economic Fluctuations: Evidence from Corporate Bond and Stock Markets," NBER working paper No. 14863.

Gjerstad, Steven and Vernon L. Smith, 2010. "Household expenditure cycles and economic cycles, 1920–2010," working paper.

Gertler, Mark and Cara Lown, 1999. "The information content of the high yield bond spread for the business cycle," *Oxford Review of Economic Policy*, Vol. 15, No. 3, pp. 132-150.

Haberler, Gottfried, 1945. "Some Observations on the Murray Full Employment Bill," *Review of Economics and Statistics*, Vol. 27, No. 3, pp. 106-109.

Hall, C.G., 1993. "An Unsearchable Providence: The Lawyer's Concept of Act of God," *Oxford Journal of Legal Studies*, Vol. 13, No. 2, pp. 227-248.

Hall, Robert E., 1999. "Labor-market frictions and employment fluctuations," in *Handbook of Macroeconomics, Vol. 1B*, eds. John B. Taylor and Michael Woodford, Elsevier Science, North-Holland: Amsterdam, (Chapter 17) pp. 1137-1170.

_____, 2010. "Why Does the Economy Fall to Pieces After a Financial Crisis?", *Journal of Economic Perspectives*, Vol. 24, No. 4, pp. 3-20.

Hamilton, James D., 1983. "Oil and the Macroeconomy since World War II," *Journal of Political Economy*, Vol. 91, No. 2, pp. 228-248.

_____, 1996. "This is What Happened to the Oil Price-Macroeconomy Relationship," *Journal of Monetary Economics*, Vol. 38, No 2, pp. 215–220.

_____, 2005. "Oil and the Macroeconomy," prepared for *The New Palgrave Dictionary of Economics*, August 24.

_____, 2009. "Causes and Consequences of the Oil Shock of 2007-08," Brookings Papers on Economic Activity (Spring), pp. 215-259.

_____, 2011. "Calling recessions in real time," *International Journal of Forecasting*, Vol. 27, No. 4, pp. 1006–1026.

Hamilton, James D. and Michael T. Owyang, 2011. "The Propagation of Regional Recessions," NBER working paper No. 16657.

Hamilton, William Peter, 1922. *The Stock Market Barometer*, Harper: New York.

Harvey, Campbell R., 1988. "Forecasts of Economic Growth From the Bond and Stock Markets," *Financial Analysts Journal*, Vol. 45, No. 5, pp. 38-45.

Hawkins, John, 2005. "Economic forecasting: history and procedures," *Economic Roundup* (Australian Treasury), autumn, pp. 1-25.

Hayek, Friedrich A., 1999. *The Collected Works of F.A. Hayek. Good Money, Part 2: The Standard, Vol. 6*, Chicago: University of Chicago Press.

Heilbroner, Robert L., [1953] 1986. *The Worldly Philosophers: The Lives, Times, and Ideas of the Great Economic Thinkers*, New York: Simon & Schuster.

Henkel, Sam James, J. Spencer Martin, and Federico Nardari, 2011. "Time-varying short-horizon predictability," *Journal of Financial Economics*, Vol. 99, No. 3, pp. 560-580.

Hernandez-Murillo, Ruben and Michael T. Owyang, 2006. "The Information Content of Regional Employment Data for Forecasting Aggregate Conditions," *Economic Letters*, Vol. 90, No. 3, pp. 335-339.

Hetzel, Robert L, 2009. "World Recession: What Went Wrong?", *Economic Affairs,* Vol. 29, No. 3, pp. 17-21.

Higgins, Byron, 1985. "Is a Recession Inevitable This Year?", *Economic Review* (Kansas City Federal Reserve), Vol. 73, No. 1, pp. 3-16.

Hirsch, Robert L., 2008. "Mitigation of maximum world oil production: Shortage scenarios," *Energy Policy*, Vol. 36, No. 2, pp. 881–889.

Hume, David, [1752] 1987. "Of Money," in *Essays, Moral, Political, and Literary*, ed. Eugene F. Miller, Indianapolis: Liberty Fund, 1987. Retrieved Jan. 18, 2012: www.econlib.org/library/LFBooks/Hume/hmMPL26.html

Hyndman, Rob J. and Yeasmin Khandakar, 2008. "Automatic Time Series Forecasting: The forecast Package for R," *Journal of Statistical Software*, Vol. 27, No. 3.

Ibbotson SBBI 2011 Classic Yearbook, 2011. Chicago: Morningstar.

Issler, Joao Victor and Farshid Vahid, 2006. "The Missing Link: Using the NBER Recession Indicator to Construct Coincident and Leading Indices of Economic Activity," *Journal of Econometrics*, Vol. 132, No. 1, pp. 281–303.

Jevons, William Stanley, 1875. "The Solar Period and the Price of Corn," in *Investigations in Currency and Finance*, London: Macmillan, 1884, pp. 194–205.

Kacapyr, Elia, 1996. *Economic Forecasting: The State of the Art*, Armonk, New York: M.E. Sharpe.

Kahneman, Daniel, 1999. "Objective Happiness," in *Well-Being: The Foundations of Hedonic Psychology*, eds. Daniel Kahneman, et al., New York: Russell Sage Foundation, 1999, pp. 3-25.

Kahneman, Daniel and Amos Tversky, 1973. "On the psychology of prediction," *Psychological Review*, Vol. 80, No. 4, pp. 237-251.

Katayama, Munechika, 2010. "Improving Recession Probability Forecasts in the U.S. Economy," working paper.

Kessel, Rueben A., 1965. "The Cyclical Behavior of the Term Structure of Interest Rates," National Bureau of Economic Research Occasional Paper No. 91.

Keynes, John Maynard, [1936] 1964. *The General Theory of Employment, Interest, And Money*, New York: Harcourt Brace.

Kim, Dong Heon, 2012. "What Is An Oil Shock? Panel Data Evidence," *Empirical Economics*, Vol. 43, No. 1, pp 121-143.

Kim, Kyun, 1988. *Equilibrium Business Cycle Theory in Historical Perspective*, Cambridge: Cambridge University Press.

King, Thomas B., Andrew T. Levin, and Roberto Perli, 2007. "Financial Market Perceptions of Recession Risk," Federal Reserve working paper No. 2007-57.

Kishor, N. Kundan and Evan F. Koenig, 2010. "Yield-Spreads as Predictors of Economic Activity: A Real-Time VAR Analysis," working paper (Federal Reserve Bank of Dallas).

Kissinger, Henry, 1982. *Years of Upheaval*, Boston: Little, Brown.

Knightly, Arthur M., 2009. "Fontainebleau Las Vegas files for Chapter 11 bankruptcy," *Las Vegas Review-Journal*, June 9.

Knoop, Todd A., 2004. *Recessions and Depressions: Understanding Business Cycles*, Westport, Connecticut: Praeger.

Koenig, Evan F., 2002. "Using the Purchasing Mangers' Index to Assess the Economy's Strength and the Likely Direction of Monetary Policy," *Economic and Financial Policy Review* (Federal Reserve Bank of Dallas), Vol. 1, No. 6, pp. 1-15.

Koopmans, Tjalling C., 1947. "Measurement Without Theory," *Review of Economics and Statistics* Vol. 29, No. 3, pp. 161-172.

Krugman, Paul, 2009. "How Did Economists Get It So Wrong," *New York Times Magazine*, Sep. 6.

Kydland, Finn E., 1993. "Business Cycles and Aggregate Labor-Market Fluctuations," working paper 9312 (Federal Reserve Bank of Cleveland).

Lahiri, Kajal and George Monokroussos, 2011. "Nowcasting US GDP: The role of ISM Business Surveys," working paper.

Lamont, Owen A., 2002. "Macroeconomic forecasts and microeconomic forecasters," *Journal of Economic Behavior & Organization*, Vol. 48, No. 3, pp. 265–280.

Laster, David, Paul Bennett, and In Sun Geoum, 1999. "Rational Bias in Macroeconomic Forecasts," *Quarterly Journal of Economics*, Vol. 114, No. 1, pp. 293-318.

Leamer, Edward E., 2007. "Housing *Is* The Business Cycle," NBER working paper No. 13428.

_____, 2008. "What's A Recession, Anyway?", NBER working paper No. 14221.

Lebergott, Stanley, 1945. "Forecasting The National Product," *American Economic Review*, Vol. 35, No. 1, pp. 59-80.

Lee, Kiseok, and Shawn Ni, and Ronald A. Ratti, 1995. "Oil Shocks and the Macroeconomy: The Role of Price Variability," *Energy Journal*, Vol. 16, No. 4, pp. 39-56.

Lefevre, Edwin, [1923] 1993. *Reminiscences of a Stock Operator*, New York: Wiley.

Levanon, Gad, Jean-Claude Manini, Ataman Ozyildirim, Brian Schaitkin, Jennelyn Tanchua, 2011. "Using a Leading Credit Index to Predict Turning Points in the U.S. Business Cycle," Conference Board Economics Program working paper No. 11-05.

Levy, David, 1993. "Interview with Robert E. Lucas Jr.," *The Region* (Federal Reserve Bank of Minneapolis), June. Retrieved Mar. 17, 2012: www.minneapolisfed.org/publications_papers/pub_display.cfm?id=3727

Liew, Jimmy and Maria Vassalou, 2000. "Can book-to-market, size and momentum be risk factors that predict economic growth?", *Journal of Financial Economics*, Vol. 57, No. 2, pp. 221-245.

Lo, Andrew W. and Jasmina Hasanhodzic, 2009. *The Heretics of Finance: Conversations with Leading Practitioners of Technical Analysis*. New York: Bloomberg Press.

Lo, Andrew W., Harry Mamaysky, and Jiang Wang, 2000. "Foundations of Technical Analysis: Computational Algorithms, Statistical Inference, and Empirical Implementation," *Journal of Finance*, Vol. 55, No. 4, pp. 1705-1756.

Loungani, Prakash, 2001, "How Accurate Are Private Sector Forecasts? Cross-country Evidence from Consensus Forecasts of Output Growth," *International Journal of Forecasting*, Vol. 17, No. 3, pp. 419-432.

Loungani, Prakash and Natalia Tamirisa, 2009. "How Well Are Recessions and Recoveries Forecast?", IMF working paper.

Lucas, Robert E., 1972. "Expectations and the Neutrality of Money," *Journal of Economic Theory*, Vol. 4, No. 2, pp. 103-124.

_____, 1976. "Econometric Policy Evaluation: A Critique," in *The Phillips Curve and Labor Markets*, eds. K. Brunner and A. Meltzer, Amsterdam: North-Holland, pp. 19-46.

_____, 2003. "Macroeconomic Priorities," *American Economic Review*, Vol. 93, No. 1, pp. 1–14.

_____, 2009. "In defence of the dismal science," *The Economist*, August 6, 2009.

Lustig, Hanno and Adrient Verdelhan, 2011. "Business Cycle Variation in the Risk-Return Tradeoff," working paper.

Mackay, Charles, [1841] 2004. *Extraordinary Popular Delusions and the Madness of Crowds*, Barnes & Noble.

Malthus, Thomas Robert, 1836. *Principles of Political Economy*, London: W. Pickering. Retrieved Jan. 24, 2012: oll.libertyfund.org/title/2188/202605 on 2012-01-24

Mankiw, N. Gregory, 2001. "The Inexorable and Mysterious Tradeoff between Inflation and Unemployment," *Economic Journal*, Vol. 111, No. 471, Conference Papers, pp. C45-C61.

_____, 2006. "The Macroeconomist as Scientist and Engineer," *Journal of Economic Perspectives*, Vol. 20, No. 4, pp. 29-46.

Marshall, Alfred and Mary Paley Marshall, 1879. *The Economics of Industry*, London: Macmillan.

Marx, Karl, [1863] 1969. *Theories of Surplus-Value: Part III*, London: Lawrence & Wishart.

_____, [1867] 1915. *Capital: A Critique of Political Economy (Vol. I: The Process of Capitalist Production)*, Chicago: Charles H. Kerr & Co.

Matsusaka, John G. and Argia M. Sbordone, 1995. "Consumer Confidence And Economic Fluctuations," *Economic Inquiry*, Vol. 33, No. 2, pp. 296–318.

Minsky, Hyman P., 1974. "The modeling of financial instability: An introduction," in *Modeling and Simulation*, 5, Proceedings of the Fifth Annual Pittsburgh Conference, Instruments Society of America, pp. 267-272.

_____, [1986] 2008. *Stabilizing An Unstable Economy*, New York: McGraw-Hill.

Mill, James, 1808. *Commerce Defended. An Answer to the Arguments by which Mr. Spence, Mr. Cobbett, and Others, have attempted to Prove that Commerce is not a source of National Wealth*, C. and R. Baldwin: London. Retrieved Jan. 20 2012: oll.libertyfund.org/title/1668.

Mill, John Stuart, [1848] 1909. *Principles of Political Economy: with some of their applications to social philosophy*, ed. William James Ashley, London: Longmans, Green and Co., 1909, 7th ed. Retrieved Jan. 23, 2012: oll.libertyfund.org/title/101

Mitchell, Wesley Clair, 1913. *Business Cycles*, Berkeley: University of California Press.

Mitchell, Wesley C. and Arthur F. Burns, 1938. "Statistical Indicators of Cyclical Revivals," Bulletin 69 (National Bureau of Economic Research), May 28.

Mody, Ashoka and Mark P. Taylor, 2003. "The High-Yield Spread As A Predictor Of Real Economic Activity: Evidence Of A Financial Accelerator For The United States," IMF Staff Papers, Vol. 50, No. 3, pp. 373-402.

Moller, Stig V. and Magnus Sander, 2013. "Stock return and dividend growth predictability across the business cycle," working paper.

Morley, James, 2010. "The Emperor Has No Clothes," *Macro Focus* (Macroeconomic Advisers), Vol. 5, No. 2.

Mullineux, A.W., 1990. *Business Cycles and Financial Crises*, Ann Arbor, Michigan: University of Michigan Press.

Murphy, David J. and Charles A. S. Hall, 2011. "Energy return on investment, peak oil, and the end of economic growth, in *Ecological Economics Reviews*, eds. Robert Costanza, Karin Limburg and Ida Kubiszewski, Annals of the New York Academy of Sciences, Vol. 1219, pp. 52-72.

Nalewaik, Jeremy J., 2011. "Forecasting Recessions Using Stall Speeds," Federal Reserve (Finance and Economics Discussion Series) working paper 2011-24.

Neely, Christopher J., et al., 2011. "Forecasting the Equity Risk Premium: The Role of Technical Indicators," Federal Reserve Bank of St. Louis working paper 2010-008E.

Newman, Philip Charles, 1952. *The Development of Economic Thought*, New York: Prentice-Hall.

Norris, Floyd, 2008. "Trump Sees Act of God in Recession," *New York Times*, Dec. 4, 2008.

Orphanides, Athanasios, 2001. "Monetary Policy Rules Based on Real-Time Data," *American Economic Review*, Vol. 91, No. 4, pp. 964-985.

Vol. 91, No. 4 (Sep., 2001), pp. 964-985

Owyang, Michael T., Jeremy M. Piger and Howard J. Wall, 2012. "Forecasting National Recessions Using State Level Data," St. Louis Federal Reserve working paper 2012-013A.

Pastor, Lubos. and Robert F. Stambaugh, 2001. "The Equity Premium and Structural Breaks," *Journal of Finance*, Vol. 56, No. 4, pp. 1207–1239.

Pearce, Douglas K., 1983. "Stock Prices and the Economy," *Federal Reserve Bank of Kansas City Economic Review*, Vol. 68, No. 9, pp. 7-22.

Perelman, Michael, 1999. *The Natural Instability of Markets: Expectations, Increasing Returns, and the Collapse of Capitalism*, New York: St. Martin's.

Petty, William, [1662] 1899. *"CHAP. IV.: Of the several wayes of Taxe, and first, of setting a part, a proportion of the whole Territory for Publick uses, in the nature of Crown Lands; and secondly, by way of Assessement, or Land-taxe,"* in *The Economic Writings of Sir William Petty, Vol. 1*, ed. Charles Henry Hull, Cambridge: Cambridge University Press, 1899. Retrieved Jan. 18, 2012: oll.libertyfund.org/titl1677/30565/1426297

Phelps, Edmund S., 1967. "Phillips Curves, Expectations of Inflation and Optimal Unemployment over Time, *Economica*, Vol. 34, No. 135, pp. 254-281.

Phillips, A. W., 1958. "The Relationship between Unemployment and the Rate of Change of Money Wages in the United Kingdom 1861-1957," *Economica*, Vol. 25, No. 100, pp. 283–299.

Pigou, Arthur C, 1927. *Industrial Fluctuations*. London: MacMillan.

Prescott, Edward C., 1986. "Theory ahead of business cycle measurement," *Federal Reserve Bank of Minneapolis Quarterly Review*, Vol. 10, No. 4, pp. 9-22.

Rapach, David E., Jack K. Strauss, and Guofu Zhou, 2010. "Out-of-Sample Equity Premium Prediction: Combination Forecasts and Links to the Real Economy," *Review of Financial Studies*, Vol. 23, No. 2, pp. 821-862.

Reid, David J., 1968. "Combining Three Estimates of Gross Domestic Product," *Economica*, Vol. 35, No. 140, pp. 431-444.

Reifschneider, David and Peter Tulip, 2007. "Gauging the Uncertainty of the Economic Outlook from Historical Forecasting Errors," Federal Reserve working paper 2007-60.

Reinhart, Carmen H. and Kenneth S. Rogoff, 2009a. "The Aftermath of Financial Crises," NBER working paper No. 14656.

_____, 2009b. *This Time Is Different: Eight Centuries of Financial Folly*, Princeton: Princeton University Press.

Ricardo, David, 2005. *The Works and Correspondence of David Ricardo (Vols. 1-11)*, ed. Piero Sraffa with the collaboration of M.H. Dobb, Indianapolis: Liberty Fund. Retrieved Jan. 24, 2012: oll.libertyfund.org/title/159

Rolnick, Art, 2010. *The Region* (Federal Reserve Bank of Minneapolis), September. Retrieved Mar. 20, 2012: www.minneapolisfed.org/publications_papers/pub_display.cfm?id=4526

Rosenberg, Joshua V. and Samuel Maurer, 2008. "Signal or Noise? Implications of the Term Premium," *Federal Reserve Bank of New York Economic Policy Review*, Vol. 14, No. 1, pp. 1-11.

Rotemberg, Julio J. and Michael Woodford, 1996. "Real-Business-Cycle Models and the Forecastable Movements in Output, Hours, and Consumption," *American Economic Review*, Vol. 86, No. 1, pp. 71-89.

Robays, Ine Van, 2012. "Macroeconomic Uncertainty and the Impact of Oil Shocks," European Central Bank working paper No. 1479.

Rudebusch, Glenn D. and John C. Williams, 2009. "Forecasting Recessions: The Puzzle of the Enduring Power of the Yield Curve," *Journal of Business and Economic Statistics*. Vol. 27, No. 4, pp. 492-503.

Say, Jean-Baptiste, [1803] 1855. *A Treatise on Political Economy; or the Production, Distribution, and Consumption of Wealth*, trans. C. R. Prinsep from the 4th ed. of the French, Philadelphia: Lippincott, Grambo & Co., 1855 (4th-5th ed.). Retrieved Jan. 23, 2012: oll.libertyfund.org/title/274

Schumpeter, Joseph, [1942] 1950. *Capitalism, Socialism and Democracy*, New York: Harper and Row.

Schwert, G. William, 1990. "Stock Returns and Real Activity: A Century of Evidence," *Journal of Finance*, Vol. 45., No. 4, pp. 1237-1257.

Sensier, Marianne, Michael Artis, Denise R. Osborna and Chris Birchenhall, 2002. "Domestic and international influences on business cycle regimes in Europe," *International Journal of Forecasting*, Vol. 20, No. 2, p. 343-357.

Sherman, Howard, 2001. "The Business Cycle Theory of Wesley Mitchell," *Journal of Economic Issues*, Vol. 35, No. 1, pp. 85-97

Shi, Shouyong, 2011. "Liquidity, Assets and Business Cycles," working paper.

Siegel, Jeremy J., 1991. "Does It Pay Stock Investors to Forecast the Business Cycle?" *Journal of Portfolio Management* (Fall), pp. 27-34.

Smith, Adam, [1776] 1981. *An Inquiry Into The Nature And Causes of the Wealth of Nations (Vols. I and II)*, Indianapolis: Liberty Fund.

Sowell, Thomas, 1972. "Sismondi: A Neglected Pioneer" *History of Political Economy*, Vol. 4, No. 1, pp. 62-88.

_____, 1974. *Classical Economics Reconsidered*, Princeton: Princeton University Press.

Stock, James H. and Mark W. Watson, 1989. "New Indexes of Coincident and Leading Economic Indicators," in *NBER Macroeconomics Annual*, Vol. 4, eds. Olivier Jean Blanchard and Stanley Fischer, Cambridge, Mass.: MIT Press, pp. 351–394.

_____, 1999. "Forecasting Inflation," *Journal of Monetary Economics*, Vol. 44, No. 2, pp. 293-335.

_____, 2003. "Forecasting Output and Inflation: The Role of Asset Prices," *Journal of Economic Literature*, Vol. 41, No. 3, pp. 788-829.

_____, 2012. "Disentangling the Channels of the 2007-2009 Recession," working paper (Brookings Panel on Economic Activity), March 22-23.

Summers, Lawrence H., 1986. "Some Skeptical Observations on Real Business Cycle Theory," *Federal Reserve Bank of Minneapolis Quarterly Review*, Vol. 10, No. 4, pp. 23-27.

Sumner, Scott, 1990. "Price-Level Stability, Price Flexibility, and Fisher's Business Cycle Model," *Cato Journal*, Vol. 9, No. 3, pp. 719-727.

_____, 2011. "Re-Targeting the Fed," *National Affairs*, No. 9, Fall, pp. 79-96.

Sustek, Roman, 2010. "Monetary aggregates and the business cycle," *Journal of Monetary Economics*, Vol. 57, No. 4, pp. 451-465.

Tainer, Evelina M., 2006. *Using Economic Indicators to Improve Investment Analysis*, Hoboken, New Jersey: Wiley.

Taleb, Nassim Nicholas, 2007. *The Black Swan: The Impact of the Highly Improbable*, New York: Random House.

Tetlock, Philip, 2005. *Expert Political Judgment: How Good Is It? How Can We Know?*, Princeton: Princeton University Press.

Thorton, Mark, 2006. "Cantillon On The Cause Of The Business Cycle," *Quarterly Journal of Austrian Economics*, Vol. 9, No. 3, pp. 45-60.

Tobin, James, 1970. "Money and Income: Post Hoc Ergo Propter Hoc?," *Quarterly Journal of Economics*, Vol. 84, No. 2, pp. 301-317.

Tsuchiya, Yoichi, 2012. "Is the Purchasing Managers' Index Useful for Assessing the Economy's Strength? A Directional Analysis," *Economics Bulletin*, Vol. 32, No. 2, pp. 1302-1311.

Tversky, Amos and Daniel Kahneman, 1974. "Judgment under Uncertainty: Heuristics and Biases," *Science*, Vol. 185, No. 4157, pp. 1124-1131.

van Suntum, Ulrich, 2005. *The Invisible Hand: Economic Thought Yesterday and Today*, Berlin: Springer.

Walrus, Leon, [1874] 1954. *Elements of Pure Economics, or The Theory of Social Wealth*, trans. W. Jaffe, Homewood, Ill.: Richard D. Irwin.

Wapshott, Nicholas, 2011. *Keynes Hayek: The Clash That Defined Modern Economics*, New York: Norton.

Weidner, Justin and John C. Williams, 2009. "How Big Is the Output Gap?," *Economic Letter* (Federal Reserve Bank of San Francisco), no. 2009-19.

Wheelock, David C., 1997. "Monetary Policy in the Great Depression and Beyond:
The Sources of the Fed's Inflation Bias," St. Louis Federal Reserve working paper 1997-011A.

Wheelock, David C. and Mark E. Wohar, 2009. "Can the Term Spread Predict Output Growth and Recessions? A Survey of the Literature," *Federal Reserve Bank of St. Louis Review*, Vol. 91, No. 5, pp. 419-440.

Wells, Donald R., 2004. *The Federal Reserve System: A History*, Jefferson, North Carolina: McFarland.

Wilcox, James A., 2008. "Consumer Sentiment and Consumer Spending," *Economic Letter* (Federal Reserve Bank of San Francisco), no. 2008-19.

Wildi, Marc, 2009. "Real-Time US-Recession Indicator (USRI): A Classical Cycle Perspective with 'Bounceback,'" working paper.

Wolfson, Martin H., 1986. *Financial Crises: Understanding the Postwar U.S. Experience*, Armonk, New York: M.E. Sharpe.

Yamarone, Richard, 2004. *The Trader's Guide to Key Economic Indicators*, New York: Bloomberg Press.

Yergin, Daniel, 1991. *The Prize: The Epic Quest For Oil, Money & Power*, New York: Simon & Schuster.

_____, 2011. *The Quest: Energy, Security, and the Remaking of the Modern World*, New York: Penguin.

Zarnowitz, Victor, 1985. "Recent work on business cycles in historical perspective," *Journal of Economic Literature*, Vol. 23, No. 2, pp. 523-580.

_____, 1986. "The Record and Improvability of Economic Forecasting," NBER working paper No. 2099.

_____, 1992. "Composite Indexes of Leading, Coincident, and Lagging Indicators," in *Business Cycles: Theory, History, Indicators, and Forecasting*, by Victor Zarnowitz, Chicago: University of Chicago Press, 1992.

Zarnowitz, Victor, and Braun, Phillip, 1993. "Twenty-two Years of the NBER-ASA Quarterly Economic Outlook Surveys: Aspects and Comparisons of Forecasting Performance," in *Business Cycles, Indicators, and Forecasting*, eds. James H. Stock and Mark W. Watson, Chicago: University of Chicago Press, 1993.

Zimmermann, Christian, 2001. "Forecasting with Real Business Cycle Models," *Indian Economic Review*, Vol. 36, No. 1, pp. 189-203.

Index

About the Author

James Picerno is a freelance journalist/analyst who specializes in topics related to the business cycle and investment strategy, including asset allocation, exchange-traded funds (ETFs) and mutual funds. Picerno is the author of *Dynamic Asset Allocation: Modern Portfolio Theory Updated For The Smart Investor* (Bloomberg Press, 2010). He also edits and publishes *The ETF Asset Class Performance Review (EACPR)*[1], a weekly newsletter that summarizes market activity for the major asset classes and their principal sub-categories. In addition, Picerno edits The Capital Spectator (CapitalSpectator.com), a finance/economics blog that's been cited by a range of news organizations, including *The Wall Street Journal*, Reuters and others. His articles have appeared in a variety of publications over the years, including *The Atlantic*, *Financial Advisor*, BankRate.com, and HorsesMouth.com. Picerno has been writing about finance and macroeconomics since the early 1990s at Bloomberg, Dow Jones and other media groups before becoming an independent writer/consultant in 2008.

---

[1] For more information about *The ETF Asset Class Performance Review,* see: www.capitalspectator.com/premium-research